SOCIETY

━━ AND ━━
SOCIAL JUSTICE:
A NEXUS IN REVIEW

SOCIETY

— AND —

SOCIAL JUSTICE:
A NEXUS IN REVIEW

BRIJ MOHAN
Louisiana State University

Foreword by

Mark Hyde
University of Plymouth, UK

With

Kripal Singh Soodan & Usha Rani Srivastava
Lucknow University

and

Sonia Kapur
University of Arkansas

iUniverse, Inc.
Bloomington

Society And Social Justice: A Nexus In Review

iUniverse books may be ordered through booksellers or by contacting:

iUniverse
1663 Liberty Drive
Bloomington, IN 47403
www.iuniverse.com
1-800-Authors (1-800-288-4677)

ISBN: 978-1-4759-0796-4 (sc)
ISBN: 978-1-4759-0797-1 (hc)
ISBN: 978-1-4759-0798-8 (ebk)

Printed in the United States of America

iUniverse rev. date: 08/14/2012

"Coming back after seven months in Indian villages, I saw the craziness of the Western world as well its capacity for rational thought."

Steve Jobs[1]

"For what right have the oppressed but one? The right to be filled with nothing but hate and contempt. And justly so, for they are kept in cages as threatening animals, forced into division, one against another—brother versus brother by sacred oppressors who, in order to maintain their security and power have denied the people of any pride, heritage, education and love. People without history or memory. A man with nothing but ignorance, hatred and amnesia is confined to the hellish reality of having no life at all. Perpetually trembling . . . trembling."[2]

Do not believe what you have heard. Do not believe in tradition because it is handed down many generations. Do not believe in anything that has been spoken of many times. Do not believe because the written statements come from some old sage. Do not believe in conjecture.

[1] Isaacson, Walter. 2011. Steve Jobs. New York: Simon & Schuster (Photo, 2 after p.328).

[2] An 'anonymous' poet cited as an epigraph in Mohan, B. *Eclipse of Freedom*, 1993: vii.

Do not believe in authority or teachers or elders. But after careful observation and analysis, when it agrees with reason and it will benefit one and all, then accept it and live by it.

Buddha (563-483 B.C.E.)

For
Neelu and Tina

Contents

Foreword

Is social justice merely an abstract ideal, forever beyond our grasp, or an end that can shape the actions of human service professionals so as to augment human welfare in morally appropriate ways? For Brij Mohan's rich corpus, the answer to this question is double-edged. Yes, the intellectual work of articulating an appropriate conception of justice is absolutely essential for without it, the work of human service professionals remains unfocussed and ineffective. But to be useful to practitioners, social justice must be articulated in ways that have practical relevance. This has been one of the key failings of much of political philosophy in the 20th Century, and beyond.

But which conception of social justice is appropriate to contemporary a circumstance that is the question? As a concept, justice has been at the heart of mainstream scholarly discourses in the allied fields of Social Policy and Social Work. One of the principal differences between Brij Mohan and this mainstream is that it relies on a monist conception of justice, or a single standard by which the human condition should be judged. For this mainstream, justice is a direct corollary of social cohesion, which requires an egalitarian distribution of material resources. Unfortunately, ideas about freedom and individual sovereignty are regarded with suspicion, even outright hostility, by this mainstream. This neglect of "the individual" has meant that the cause of freedom has been monopolized by Neoliberalism, which is hostile to social justice. Brij Mohan's pioneering work addresses this omission by articulating a pluralist conception of justice, recognizing the vital importance of material equality and individual autonomy.

At the center of Brij Mohan's analysis is his insistence that the public authority has a vital role to play in securing the conditions that make individual autonomy possible. Without this egalitarian foundation, individual freedom and choice translate into alienation and despair, providing a fertile breeding ground for totalitarian political movements. Yet without appropriate individual rights and enforcement mechanisms, the public authority may itself become a substantial threat to individual autonomy. Far from dismissing individual freedom as an irrelevant pre-occupation of neoliberalism, then, Brij Mohan's work shows how "the individual" must be at the heart of social justice. If it is to contribute in a meaningful way to the attainment of justice, the work of human services professionals must embrace individual autonomy as a central guiding principle.

The intellectual rigor, breadth of vision, and penetrating insights of one of the World's leading social work intellectuals has never been more clearly demonstrated than in this remarkable Magnum Opus.

Mark Hyde
Professor in Public Policy and Management
Plymouth Business School
University of Plymouth, Plymouth, United Kingdom

October 25, 2011

PREFACE

Virginia Wolfe once said, "It's no joke to write a book." A book on one's own books is more than the sum of its total; and, believe me, it's no joke! This omnibus seeks to offer randomized cross-sectional representation of my life's work. The multi-linearity of certain constructs that run through an opus is carefully combed to situate the essence of a protean trajectory encompassing an array of issues broadly classified in five thematic areas. Unlike any festschrifts, it's a self-reflective anthology of my views, constructs and conceptions of varied social phenomena and realities. The idea of such a book was first offered by my esteemed friend and colleague Professor Priscilla Allen[3].

It's my hope that students, researchers, policy makers, administrators, and intellectuals will find this compendium helpful to comprehend integrative complexity of social phenomena and the need to apply their intuitive imagination. As an anthological compilation, this book might serve as a *Brij Mohan Reader* as well. Since most of my books are solo monographs, their universal availability all at once is an unrealistic expectation for students and teachers who might look for original sources.

A writer can never be the best judge of his work; I leave my finger prints all over my writings. Whereas I am painfully aware of my limitations, I am deeply conscious of the causes that are dear to my heart, mind and soul.

To the best my knowledge there is no such book on a range of intertwined subjects by a single writer in our field. As such no existing anthology or reader in social welfare (comparative social

---

3   Allen, Priscilla D. 2010. Brij Mohan by himself. *Journal of Comparative Social Welfare*, 26, 2-3: 93-98.

policy and development) compares this volume. Some of the quotes embody my "eureka" moments; several others are brought to my attention by students, friends, reviewers, and co-editors of this volume. After a rough patch, working on this volume was both refreshing and rewarding.

I would like to thank Professors Christian Aspalter, Thomas D. Watts, Lilly Allen and many other friends who inspired me to undertake this project more than once. I am equally grateful to Kirpal, Usha and Sonia, the coeditors, who helped me put together some relevant observations with unselfish care and uncanny talents. *The flaws in design, structure and substance are solely owed to my own imperfections.*

We have remained within the "fair use" limits of citations. For the record, permissions were sought from all publishers with assured acknowledgments. It seems a few publishers are completely inaccessible. I have heard nothing from a few old publishers. However, I remain indebted to all, especially those who generously granted permission. It's with great pleasure that I acknowledge my indebtedness to Palgrave Macmillan, New York; ABC-CLIO, LLC, Santa Barbara; Routledge (T&F), UK and Schenkman, Rochester, NY.

After a great deal of consideration, I chose i-Universe to be my publisher. A new culture of glossy textbooks and celebrity publishing with obscenely high advanced royalties has nearly destroyed the possibility of bringing out a writer's omnibus who has not been endorsed by Oprah Winfrey. Self-publication is a principled protest against the vulgar realities of commercially privileged publishing. I am grateful to Mr. Steven Cortez, Jill Serinas and Ms. Mars Alma at i-Universe who helped me bring this project out in a timely, professional manner. Eduardo M. Perez has invested his time and imagination to help design the cover photographs. It's my fourth book that carries his creative signatures. I am grateful to him and the LSU Public Relations for their courtesies.

With profound love and gratitude, I dedicate this book in honor of my daughters, Neelu and Tina.

Brij Mohan
January 23, 2012

PROLOGUE

Once a generous reviewer graciously commented:
"Mohan brings many other definitions for the concept of social welfare. This reviewer feels like a pearl-diver because every page contains so many gems that should be shared, discussed, and than serve as guides for action. Consider, for example, the following:

'. . . social welfare is a guilt-reduction mechanism for the casualties of modernity and industrialism. The state, therefore, is morally obligated to redeem itself through redistributive justice' (Mohan, 1988: 55)[4]

I was tremendously encouraged to zoom back and read my own work. It was not an easy task. Some of my good friends had previously suggested to anthologize a book of my favorite pieces from different books to offer a window on the totality of my work. A project that looked so simple was confounded by personal hesitation and modesty rather than its complexity. Reluctantly, however, I took on the galling challenge with great humility in the interest of my work and its relevance for the future.

I was not sure how to assemble a collage of quotes with an archeologist's instinct. A thematic, selective but inclusive approach looked feasible despite conceptual underpinnings that ran through the entire interdisciplinary stream. The compendium that emerged is not at all a complete or exhaustive representation of my whole work.

---

[4]   Loewenberg, Frank M. Review of *The Logic of Social Welfare: Conjectures and Formulations*. New York: St. Martin's 1988 in *Journal of International and Comparative Social Welfare*, May 1989, 5, 1: 45-47.

Ever since 'social' prefixed 'science', the spirit of the Enlightenment has been our guiding light. It's almost counterfactual to think of a world without social injustice. Society is an abstraction; its transformation is a reality. We may and may not ever achieve equality and justice but the ideas of social justice will always distinguish us from animals. Social Work is not a science; it's professional enterprise, an art of practicing hope (Mohan 2003). D.H. Lawrence brilliantly wrote: "Truly art is a sort of subterfuge .. .. The artist usually sets out—or used to—to point out a moral and adorn a tale. The tale, however, points the other way, as a rule. Two blankly opposing morals, the artist's and the tale's. Never trust the artist. Trust the tale. The proper function of a critic is to save the tale from the artist who created it ([1923] 1971: 2; emphasis added)[5].

This book was initially designed to appear as Agony and Ecstasy as an embodiment of my Omnibus. For many a good reason, I have changed the book title. This critique in review posits five main thematic elements that social scientists, especially social work educators and practitioners, confront in transformative practice. The crisis of "human-social development" (Mohan 2007) reinforces a need for exploring the society-justice nexus in a diversely complicated world. While certain prescriptive frameworks, observations and guidelines are proffered with humility, I still don't know what the answers are to this civilization's monumental failures. I hope my students will find a way out of this paralytic-axiological dissonance. I do not expect much from the professoriate. A noble profession has been transformed into its own nemesis by a Circean circle, if you will. They are true "artists" in specious occupations; perhaps, omens of a false dawn.[5]

---

[5]   Lawrence, D.H. ([1923] 1971) Studies in Classic American Literature. New York: The Viking Press.

A simple taxonomy of this omnibus is vaguely organized around a constellation of five major sections. Each part opens with an introductory narrative that contextualizes the essence and ethos of varied human conditions.

I. The Human Condition
II. Theoretico-Philosophical Streams
III. Social Constructs and Interventions
IV. International Aspects and Issues
V. Science, Society, and Values

Methodology: Process and Parameters[6]

The citations selected for this volume are assembled according to the classificatory system presented above. This will allow readers to locate and access appropriate themes from most of my publications. If developed into a comprehensive system, the quantum of analyses would involve several doctoral dissertations. As a substitute for this possibility, this book may well serve as a guide to unraveling the symbiotic dynamic of social and psychological phenomena which has been the burden of my work.

The five categories which classify a range of topics include concepts and constructs that have been developed and used to reflect on numerous human conditions as a framework. There is no rational basis for creating these separate sections as it tends to fracture the very basis of wholeness and holistic thinking. However, we made these taxonomical subsections and categories to spread out distinct but related subjects from a pragmatic viewpoint.

Since most of the citations are quoted from my sixteen books included in the Bibliography, the abbreviated references parenthetically refer to year of publication/s and their page numbers. This eliminates the formal requirement of repeatedly citing the

---

[6] All quotes are from my published books. The Bibliography includes only the ones that are actually cited in this omnibus. http://www.socialwork.lsu.edu/html/facultystaff/faculty/mohan.html

same name (author) with wasteful monotony. For example, if there is a quote from *Development, Poverty of Culture and Social Policy*, its corresponding citation will appear in parenthesis as (*DPoC&SP*, 2011: page number/s). Other contextually relevant sources beyond these books have been appropriately footnoted.

A Bibliography in Context

1. 2011. *Development, Poverty of Culture and Social Policy.* New York: Palgrave Macmillan. (DPoC&SP)
2. 2007. *Fallacies of Development: Crises of Human and Social Development.* New Delhi: Atlantic Pub. (FoD)
3. 2005. *Reinventing Social Work: Reflections on the Metaphysics of Social Practice.* Lewiston, NY: Edwin Mellen. (RSW)
4. 2003. *The Practice of Hope.* Philadelphia: Xlibris (Random House) (PoH)
5. 2002. *Social Work Revisited.* Philadelphia, PA: Xlibris (SWR)
6. 1999. *Unification of Social Work: Rethinking Social Transformation.* Westport, CT: Praeger. (UoSW)
7. 1996. *Democracies of Unfreedom.* Westport, CT: Praeger. (DoU)
8. 1993. *Eclipse of Freedom: The World of Oppression.* Westport, CT: Praeger. (EoF)
9. 1992. *Global Development: Post-Material Values and Social Praxis.* New York: Praeger. (GD:PMV&SP)
10. 1989. (Ed) *Glimpses of International and Comparative Social Welfare.* Canberra: IFSED, Inc. (GoI&CSW)
11. 1988. *The Logic of Social Welfare: Conjectures and Formulations.* New York: St. Martin's. (LoSW)
12. 1987. *Denial of Existence: Essays on the Human Condition.* Springfield, IL: Charles C Thomas. (DoE)
13. 1985a. (Ed) *Toward Comparative Social Welfare.* Cambridge, MA: Schenkman. (TCSW)
14. 1985b. (Ed) *New Horizons of Social Welfare and Policy.* Cambridge, MA: Schenkman. (NHoSW)

15. 1973. *Social Psychiatry in India: A Treatise on the Mentally Ill.* Calcutta: Minerva. (SPiI)
16. 1972. *India's Social Problems: Analyzing Basic Issues.* Allahabad: Indian International Publications. (ISP)

Founding Editor-in-Chief, *Journal of Comparative Social Welfare,* (JCSW, 1985-2011)

I

The Human Condition

"What I call *le vécu* is the accumulation of the dialectical process of psychic life insofar as this process remains obscure to itself as a constant totalization. It is impossible to be conscious of a totalization which also totalizes consciousness. *Le vécu,* in this sense, is permanently susceptible of comprehension but never of knowledge."

Jean Paul Sartre (quoted by his biographer.[7])

Key Concepts

Alienation • Social Theory and the Human Condition; the Human Reality; Exclusion; Existential Intervention • Mental Illness • Oppression • Violence and Counter Violence •Terror, Terrorism and Counter-Terrorism • Caste and Casteism

Le vécu offered me a new critical perspective to comprehend and think outside the box. The human condition, thus, has been the general foundation of my conceptual framework. In doing so, Franco-German thoughts, especially Continental Philosophy, has been my main theoretical endowment. While Gandhian thought

---

[7]   Hayman, Ronald. 1987. *Sartre: A Life.* New York: Simon and Schuster, p. 431.

has guided my moral orientation, Sartrean ethics and dialectical reason have empowered my intellectual thrusts to analyze different aspects and issues relative to human conditions.

Since I was born and raised in India, I have been especially sensitive to the oppression of the poor and down trodden in general, especially about *Dalit*. After 1975, I found African and Mexican Americans in similar conditions in the United States. Professionally I began scientific exploration of subjects like mental illness soon after my Master's education in social work (1960). As I grew, I began to recognize the universal chains that enslave us in a myriads of dehumanizing conditions.

Michel Foucault's "madness" escaped me until the onset of eighties; my consciousness had remained eclipsed under Freudian loyalty. When I came to know his archeology of knowledge, it did not surprise me to find a Sartrean kin in him. Having published a book on Social Psychiatry (1973) and numerous papers in mental health journals, I finally realized the phony dichotomy between sanity and insanity, a false duality institutionalized by the DSM architects. No wonder DSM5 still remains disputed under the clouds of conceptual conundrums and therapeutic politics[8].

I found the world outside mental institutions much more chaotic and sick than what I had studied in the dreary wards of those asylums (1972; 1973). After more than four decades of dialogical teaching and reflective research, I have sadly discovered the *poverty of culture* (PoC) at the heart of our continued misfortunes. *Poverty of Culture* (Mohan, 2011) unravels the dynamics of our cultural meltdowns. One may agree with me or not but certain inconvenient 'absolutes' warrant new interpretations. My search for freedom, encompassing unfreedoms unleashed by oppressive cultures and predatory institutions, continues (Mohan 1985 to 2011). A 'comparative-analytic' framework (1985a and1985b) did help me situate and interconnect spatio-temporal "dots" beyond the disciplinarities of dated dogmas.

---

[8]   *See* Clud, John. What counts as crazy? *Time,* March, 19, 2012: 2-45.

Essence and Ethos: Citations

"From the Wall Street meltdown to the catastrophic manmade disasters, one discerns the invisible hand of human avarice and audacity, which make life needlessly difficult for the future generations. . . . Modernization involves application of science, technology, reason to our day-to-day affairs . . . [M]y intent is to underscore arrogance as the source of our continued anxiety, avarice, and alienation."

DPoC&SP (2011: xiii)

"The author calls for *Enlightenment II*, a new epoch in the evolution of human history promoting counter-hegemonic analyses, policies and programs. In a hopelessly divided world, the re-emergence of barriers and walls, ubiquity of terror and counter-terror, and pervasive malaise of arrogance will not deliver a world without the scourges of poverty, intolerance and war. It's not the culture of poverty, it's the poverty of culture that continues to bedevil humanity. The flickers of *New Social Development* offer a way out of the paralysis of hope that thwarts human and social progress."

DPoC&SP (2011: 28)

"Humankind's greatest challenges are still confounded by a hydra of 'inconvenient' truths that threaten essential conditions of life: security (*terrorism*), economy (*fiscal insecurity*), environment (*global warming*), human development (*bigotry, disease, and poverty*). Developmental perspective has failed to liberate humanity from the scourges of age old evils."

DPoC&SP (2011: 31)

"A hedonist culture wallowing in hubristic delusions is bound to crash. The contradictions of a society based on unprincipled consumption and consumerism is a bad news for the future of humankind."

DPoC&SP (2011: 48)

"Ideological bias and theoretical predilections of Schools and individuals vitiate the purpose, content and method of research. Scientism on the one hand and heuristic orientations on the other tend to distort free inquiry and its impact. The outcome is intellectual territoriality, social exclusion and cognitive dogmatism. University research units must eschew these temptations; institutional-individual narcissism poisons academic climate and a sort of new "fundamentalism" tends to pervade the entire research culture."

DPoC&SP (2011: 18)

"If the fall of Berlin Wall and dissolution of the Soviet Union were the most important events of the late twentieth century, the rise of China and India is the most significant development of the 21st Century so far (p. 65) . . . . Democracy has become a euphemism for diverse interest groups with disguised hegemonic interests (p. 71) . . . . We live in a warrior culture . . . . The problem has been confounded by the murderous politics of new fundamentalism. This is equally unfortunate that Asia will continue to suffer more on account of the omnipotence of the faiths founded by the three sons of Abraham. This does not bode well as prescient to a world without violence, terror and war. The basic challenges still remain unanswered by both tradition and modernity (p. 73).

DPoC&SP (2011: 65-73)

"In the Age of Reason, unreason prevails as a pervasive reality. This human paradox is irrational at best, self-destructive at worst. The advancement of science and technology especially in fields that relate to human wellbeing has brought paradigmatic changes but ghosts continue to haunt, guns remain loaded and gods remain active in search of hideously wrong pursuits."

DPoC&SP (2011: 111)

"The oppressive states with inbuilt structure of exclusion, punishment and torture have served as engines of anti-state terror (p.90) . . . . Let's revisit the archeology of some colonial oppression, its devastating legacy and counterproductive consequence . . . Narendra Singh Sarila . . . has produced a mountain of documents which unravel the "untold story of India's partition" under *The Shadows of the Great Game* (2006). He concludes: **"Many of the roots of Islamic terrorism sweeping the world today lie buried in the partition of India"** (2006: 11; emphasis added). History and counter-history present two different stories. Martyrs and terrorists also depict the same irony. "

DPoC&SP (2011: 90-91)

"Caste as a system of stratified inequality has globally survived in different forms since times immemorial. Its functionality on the subcontinent, however, is sustained by a mythologized social reality that runs contrary to the ideals of social democracy (p. 97) . . . . The more I tried to learn , the more I got alienated from my own tradition. More than 30 years ago, when I migrated to a new "promised land," I found similar, if not the same, exclusions with alarming contradictions in a nation founded in the name of freedom (p. 98)."

DPoC&SP (2011: 97-98)

"When irrationality is wedded to arrogance, stupidity is born . . . . I would argue that the dichotomy of developed and developing nations is a meaningless absurdity . . . . A new consciousness to deconstruct the existing culture of violence, alienation, and institutional-individual narcissism calls for a paradigm shift that essentially boils down to certain basic rules of civility. A responsible society must promote and sustain the elemental humanity of each individual and community. This seems to be better, perhaps the only, way to transform the world."

Social Development Issues (2011, 33, 3: 74-77)

"When certain individuals and groups are subjected to unkind beliefs (*isms*) and unfair practices (discrimination), ideology becomes a tool of oppression. Nazism of the nadir of this behavior . . . . While prejudice is prejudged negative attitude, discrimination is an act of villainy. Both serve as tools in the oppressive hands of a perpetrator who discriminates others on the basis of caste, class, race, gender, age, origin, and beliefs."

EoF (1993: 56)

"Our belief systems generate the ideologies of freedom and oppression . . . . When a person or a class of persons act(s) as perpetrator(s) . . . . we speak of an oppressive situation . . . . When societal institutions become barriers of equality and justice—the two guardians of true freedom (Mohan, 1988)—human oppression becomes pervasive evil. In brief, this is the anatomy of unfreedom."

EoF (1993: 56-57)

"Social theory attempts to unravel areas of social reality creatively analyzing the world we live in. Ideology merely galvanizes a preferred perspective. The human condition, a focal subject of analytical reasoning, becomes a canvas vulnerable to ideological stokes. The reconstruction of social reality calls for an evaluative-emancipatory analysis of social structures and human behaviors beyond the Freud-Marx and the Parsons-Habermas paradigms."

GoI&CSW (1989: 7-8)

"Dimensions of human freedom and unfreedom constitute the crux of all human conditions. Freedom is an awesome responsibility and unfreedom is a vicious trap. Man's enslavement is an outcome of his own needs, trappings, and artifacts."

DoE (1987: 3)

"Human conditions are adaptations to social reality over which mortals have lost control. Science and technology have ceased to be—perhaps they never were! —liberating forces. Civilization is a slaughterhouse. Commercialization of the cosmos has cost the scientists and the universe the ultimate value: Human dignity."

DoE (1987: 3)

"The analysis of the human condition transcends the rigid premises of behaviorism, scientism, and system –oriented perspectives because objectivity, quantification and value-freedom do not adequately explain the nature and dimension of human suffering . . . . Experience, consciousness, and wholeness are essential ingredients of human conditions that determine the nature of existence as lived through differential processes. Behavioral sciences, in their reliance on quantification and mathematical rigor, represent a flight from [human] reality."

DoE (1987: 5)

"Existential intervention is conceptualized here as a viable outlook for the alleviation of human suffering in a self-creative dialectical process. It helps rebuild the impaired identity . . . . It highlights one fundamental value: the impairing of self is remediable though an existential process involving realistic self-appraisal, awareness and actualization, directional-reorientation, and experiential-cognitive modes. . . . A new principle in existential social work is formulated: it brings into focus a therapeutic quest for the emergence of an integrative identity beyond the client-centered systems."

DoE (1987: 28)

Domestic violence is kind of silent social plague; its dimensions are complex and staggering. Vanishing familial ties, across cultural and regional boundaries, represent the malaise of the ailing social systems. A wounded family corrodes societal conscience."

DoE (1987: 61)

"Asylum-like horrid conditions of the mental hospitals at work, appalling magnitude of mental ills, staggering lack of proper therapeutic programs, callously negative community attitudes towards the poor insane and—above all—the general socio-economic conditions of a painfully acquisitive feudally oriented system, present both a challenge and an opportunity to all those concerned with the task of nation-building to work out a rationally conceived integrated plan of action inspired with a progressive ideology directed toward the welfare of the mentally ill in India."

SPiI (1973: 2)

". . . [M] ental illness and mental health are not absolute conditions; the former becomes distinguishable when the desired attributes of the latter appear disappearing. While impairment affecting role and status calling for psychiatric attention helps us define mental illness, personal maturity marked by adequate socio-personal adjustment, integration, self-restraint, reality orientation and cultural adaptability enables the identification of positive attributes that characterize mental health. In social psychiatry both conditions need to be studied in togetherness. This opens unlimited vistas of collaboration between the psychiatrist and the social scientist."

SPiI (1973:13)

"Caste system, the fundamental rhythm of Indian life, is the genesis of casteism and untouchability. . . . Indeed it is a basis of social stratification. . . . The division of human groups on the basis of disposition, character and capacity is a general characteristic of most societies, particularly those feudally stratified. Caste in India seems to be the essence of social structure and its survival as its all pervasive influence characterizes the very Indian way of life."

ISP (1972: 21)

"The revolt of Harijans[9] appears imminent against the tyranny of the high castes. . . . The provision of reserved constituency for scheduled castes is a calculated attempt to keep the lower castes divided amongst themselves. A faction-ridden community would find it well neigh impossible to win over its enemy. It is a greater challenge for the Harijans; their dilemma will continue unless they rid themselves of bourgeoization. This is, however, a revolutionary task and [it] cannot be accomplished with mere obsessive notions and slogans . . . . To eradicate casteism and untouchability a caste war has to be fought no doubt but its ideology and program of action should be objectively progressive.

---

[9] 'Dalit' is now a preferred concept to refer to all oppressed lower castes including the 'scheduled' ones.

It would be self-defeating and nationally devastating to resort to reactionary methods and thinking."[10]

ISP (1972: 27; 28-29)

"The eclipse of civility spells the dualism of despair and hope. Human oppression is an inescapable experience. The pain of huger is no more a Third World curse; scourges of poverty and authoritarianism are pervasive. Even the most advanced nations in the world are not immune to the ravages of the new poverty—a phenomenon that marks the failure of the post-industrial society in meeting common human needs."

EoF (1993: xi)

"Oppression has no identity; it's the ugly name of a feckless behavior born out of human rapaciousness, compulsions, and manipulative power which I prefer to call *predatory politics*. Equally, perhaps more, indomitable is the human urge to breathe the fresh air of freedom."

EoF (1993: xi)

"The triumph of global capitalism is sadly based on the every-man-for-himself doctrine. Amid the ambiguities of the twentieth century post-war climate one finds that brutality still works. The archaic elements of human nature still regulate the conduct, which falls short of civilized behavior. However, the only organizing principle that keeps the societal cauldron from spilling [over] seems to be the powerlessness of the oppressed

---

[10]   The prescience of these observations is however notable. The revolt of the Dalit has changed the contours of national politics. In states like Uttar Pradesh, which has been ruled by a 'Dalit' woman, Mayawati, it is reflective of a widespread corruption of revolutionary praxis.Not that things have changed after Mulayam Singh, her nemesis, replaced her of late. India's current caste war is reactionary at best.

people. How else could one explain the invincibility of the authority of whose legitimacy remains in question? The state benefits from, and depends on, the functional rationale of its coercive power."

EoF (1993: xii)

"The ravages of postmodern crisis challenge the development and education of the human animal—an incomplete creature in search of a meaningful identity. Exploration of this unfreedom is but a step toward becoming universally free."

EoF (1993: xii)

"Despite a nebulous description, human oppression remains an encompassing ontological reality.... Human experience as a datum merits a phenomenological inquiry should oppression be the prism of policy directions. Societal institutions have traditionally sought to safeguard human dignity against the vagaries of nature and individual-social circumstances. Frequently, however, social arrangements and human nature fail to promote freedom and become tools of oppression. Human struggle for, and beyond, survival is a perennial saga of liberation from the innate trappings and external barriers."

EoF (1993: xv)

"Our social world is a smorgasbord of human duality; its paradoxes and contradictions signify the intersection between rational and irrational, external and temporal, material and metaphysical."

EoF (1993: xv)

"Racism is as American as apple pie. Hostility and contempt based on the color of human skin is not a new phenomenon, however. India's 'varnavyavastha'—system based on color—the cornerstone of "casteism," is a primal form of racism that has sustained the egalitarian reforms of a modern democracy."

EoF (1993: 57)

"The paradox of Enlightenment has created islands of knowledge that represent fractured realities. The post-industrial explosion of technological advancements has further confounded this distorted human reality. Strides of meta-information alone have created a 'cybertribal[11]' schizophrenic reality that calls for the reinvention of science, values, and relationships."

UoSW: RSR (1999: xii)

"Caring and sharing nurture a civil-responsible order. Modern social workers have scientific knowledge and tools to alleviate social problems. As specialists they perform complex functions offering problem/population-specific services in a host of settings . . . they seek to professionalize the whole problem-solving process."

UoSW: RSR (1999: xiii)

"Despite phenomenal philanthropic altruism, the horrors of poverty and deprivation continue to dehumanize the oppressed people . . . . In social work the Flexner myth has continually sustained a heated debate on the subject. While a group of overconfident practitioners have . . . found comfort in their self-acclaimed success, critical thinkers in the profession continue to question the mission, method, and mythologies surrounding the notions of help, service, and the professional excellence."

UoSW: RSR, (1999: ix)

---

[11]   My letter to the Editor, *Time,* September 15, 1997: 18.

"Terrorism and counter-terrorism constitute a nexus of evil: Terrorism is one of the ugly faces or evil; counter-terrorism is vile reaction to evil which sustains both evilness and its villainy. When state and its agents become instruments of terror, it leads to the moral dissolution of its legitimacy. Terrorism has its roots in annihilating suffocation, blind rage, unexamined faith, unkind beliefs and lack of both rationality and humanity. Counter-terrorism derives its strength from its own nefarious motives and tools. To distinguish between the two one must critically analyze the dynamics that breed terror, arrogance, hopelessness and violence."

FoD: CoH&SD (1997: 36-37)

Conclusion

Alienation is an inalienable dimension of the human condition. Keats' 'negative capability' is crucial to comprehend this aspect of human-social reality. I have made a modest attempt to theorize certain facets of such unfreedoms that dehumanize people all over the world.

II

THEORETICO-PHILOSOPHICAL STREAMS

"How painfully confused the cultured men of such era must be to behold a phenomenon that can only be grasped by comparison with the very Hellenic genius that they have never understood — the reawakening of the Dionysiac spirit and the rebirth of tragedy? In no other artistic age have socalled 'culture' and art itself been so mutually hostile as we see them today."

Friedrich Nietzsche[12]

Key Concepts

Existentialism • Freudo-Marxist Endowment • Logical Humanism • Philosophy as Practice • Non-Western Social Thoughts • Post-Material Praxis

My father was a physician, philosopher and philanthropist—a dangerous combination that permeated his rise and fall as a worldly man. Above all, he was a wise and noble human being. Though we lived in relative poverty, despite his good medical practice, ancestral assets and his creative mind, family values with empathetic orientation and altruistic attitudes transformed my whole view of material wealth and its significance. *All property is a theft*—looked to

---

[12] *The Birth of Tragedy.* Tans. Shaun Whiteside. London: Penguin Books, 1993:97.

be a very accurate definition and source of inequality, as I understood reality as a young student.

In this family milieu of modest means and a heightened sense of religious morality, I grew up as a rebel with a cause. When throngs of impoverished patients arrived early morning at my father's clinic with their dying infants, I realized there was something terribly wrong somewhere. Why only poor ones had to suffer on account of misery for which they were not responsible? For a while I followed my father's philosophy of Karma and dharma but it did not help me much. As soon as I began to develop my own sense of logic and ethics, I questioned the hollow righteousness of our religious culture. In one of our earliest family visits to the temples of Vrindaban, I noted how Dalits were excluded from entrance. I plainly disagreed with my father about god's authority who would distinguish between classes and discriminate against the poor "untouchables." My journey had begun on a rather tedious track. After graduation, I joined Master of Social Work, a new program at Agra University. My sense of social work then was more pragmatic than philosophical. It was my assumption that MSWs could be the next messiahs of social change as India was embarking upon a massive national social development program through its Five Years Plans.

I moved to Lucknow University to benefit from the tutelage of celebrated scholars at a prestigious University, a pioneer in higher education where social work at doctoral level was offered for the first time in any university beyond the U.S. (to the best of my knowledge). It offered me the opportunity to explore human conditions—their dynamics— which were bubbling up in a young restless mind. The field work involved interviewing and observing hospitalized mental patients in the three mental hospitals of North India (UP). To date that experience stands out as the peak of my learning. The more I knew about mental illness, the less I knew about "normal" human behavior. With humility and sustained interest, I continue to explore human dimensions of social misery without a convincing recipe for radical transformation. As a natural evolutionary process, in my quest for a paradigm that unfolds patinas of difficult issues, I continue to seek answers to knotty questions with a sense of philosophical angst and hope. If this sounds escapist, I offer my apology. I have to believe that practice of ethical norms with a philosophical approach to personal and social problems serves both as a tranquilizer and prophylaxis for undue pain and unwarranted anguish. This approach does not help you to fight corruption in India and stop genocide in South Sudan; this does help you to practice hope with a creative attitude in an otherwise chaotic world.

If social and natural scientists would embrace each other without orthodoxies of their calling, theoretical-scientific interpretations would tremendously enhance the cause of human liberation. It's not ignorance; it's the arrogance of the learned that worries me most. Anti-dialogic disciplinarities sabotage knowledge and its interpretations. A philosophical orientation is crucial to relate to others, the "others' whom we tend to neglect, abuse, dread and hate. When I say there is only one race, i.e., the human race, I behold humanity as a family, which has become dysfunctional at best.

Some of the relevant constructs that represent these formulations are best analyzed and discussed in three specific books: *Global Development: Post-Material Values and Social Praxis* (1992); *The Practice of Hope* (2003) and *Reinventing Social Work* (2005). I will walk you through some of these resources.

Essence and Ethos: Citations

"The rise of capitalism is not the threat; it's a great impetus for the engines of growth and prosperity. The real dangers are however inbuilt in the obsolence of its innovations howsoever beneficial and pragmatic they seem. The flawed structure, design and operations of both macro and micro economics have nearly brought the world economy to its knees. The same is true of its ideological shibboleths, fads and offshoots. Some people may get Nobel prizes for these ideas but these individual triumphs are no indicators of truth and discovery."

DPoC&SP (2011: 8)

"Developmentalism as movement is rooted in our neo-Darwinian neurosis against the socialist aspirations of the "undeveloped" world euphemistically re-baptized as *developing nations*[13]. Social development, like social work, has been a hegemonic approach to serve counter-revolutionary purpose (*See* Easterly, 2007; Klein, 2007; Haque, 1999; and Smith, 1985). Social theorists saw this as a system of interdisciplinary approach to unravel the interdependence and interaction amongst different societies (Geertz, 1963; Parsons and Shils, 1962). It nearly matched the time when the notion of the Welfare State gained credence from Parsonian macro functionalism (Gouldner, 1970). In other words, developmentalism emerged as a western recipe for the functionality of the dysfunctional *third world*. Interestingly, social welfare as an institution served the same function in the West: meeting revolution half-way in the post post-war industrial societies".

DPoC&SP (2011: 32)

"We must first look inside the box before we reconnect the dots outside the box."

JCSW, 2012, 28 (1: 78)

"The main burden of these musings is to underscore the foundational significance of post-Nietzschean-Darwinian-Sartrean streams of thought that have deconstructed the meaning of *being* and *becoming* as a paradigm shift in our understanding of human nature and behavior . . . . I believe *postmodern* is a

---

[13] The Global South, the Third World, has been the focus of developmentalist model creating a conceptual hiatus between "traditional" and "modern" societies. This neo-colonial approach was developed in the name of democracy to open free markets as a shield against the rise of communism.

misnomer. . . . The rise of anti-Platonism lent support to anti-essentialism, which has helped develop postmodern thought in arts, humanities and literature. In social/human services, its impact has been monumental without a clearer understanding of its meaning, implication, and impact"

Journal of Social Work Education (2011, 47.3: 620-624)

"The importance of the *noise source* needs no emphasis. Modernity has exposed its wounds and vulnerabilities. Its Achilles' tendon makes us rethink about the Enlightenment that fed us sugar-coated pills in the name of scientific growth and social engineering. Human and social developments represent the symbiosis of a successful society devoid of unfreedom."

FoD: CHSD (2007: xi)

"Optimism without an empathetic sense of reality is an apology to cultivated somnambulism. The post-industrial society—in the throes of a variegated crisis—is like an orphan, if not aborted, child whose mother [modernity] did not get the midwife's help."

EoF (1993: 5)

"The idea of *Philosophy as Practice* is by no means my invention . . . . If politicization of science is an inevitable fact of post-industrial society, how can philosophy remain unaffected by the epistemological pollution hovering over the temples of learning?"

RSW: RMSP (2005: 4-5)

"I will attempt to lay down a basic framework of *Philosophy as Practice* paradigm in my hope to legitimize its disciplinarity with a purpose: Philosophy as a vehicle of social transformation (Mohan, 1999;

2003). Three *a priori* assumptions undergird this formulation:

- Objectivity is essentially an inter-subjective construct;
- Scientificity and humanity are not necessarily antithetical; and
- Philosophy as practice can redeem itself as a vehicle of human liberation.

RSW: RMSP (2005: 5)

"The salience of this proposition is marked by three factors which signify the *Philosophy as Practice* perspective. First, the new anxiety factor which involves fear and depression about mundane aspects of life ranging from job insecurity to terrorist attack. Second, failure of science to eschew its organizational needs in favor of scientific truth; and third, the butterfly effect. The last one is a futuristic vision to change the world as we see it; catastrophe theory lends support to its validity."

RSW: RMSP (2005: 5-6)

"I will follow dialectical method to delineate the areas that I deem appropriate for philosophical practice. What is anti-philosophical is marked by [its] innate malignancy.... Still more important is to demythologize the orthodoxy of the scientific method that reinforces a culture of exclusion."

RSW: RMSP (2005: 7)

"There is a new surge of theocentric curricula, books, music, films and other pedagogical and mainstream entertainment tools usually masquerading under the banner of *spirituality*. One's faith, or lack of it, does not necessarily make him/her *philosophical* and/ or *spiritual*. Also, it's dangerous to legitimize religion as a philosophical domain despite a clear grey area between the two. An unbeliever may also be a great philosopher-practitioner."

RSW: RMSP (2005: 7)

Conclusion

Professionalism dictates that we undergird theory and practice with sound theoretical bases. Pragmatic expedience and wallmartization of knowledge and diplomas have thawrted the growth of fundamental principles of our calling. The entire learning-teaching spectrum of social work education is almost philosophically illiterate and, as a consequence, anti-intellectual. A new textbook culture patronized by our leading professional organizations and commercial publishers have nearly killed the art of independent scholarship that sustained and promoted original works. The result is bastardized models and recycled texts have replaced intellectual habits that nourished creative minds. Do we still need such texts at the expense of students? The mushroom growth of on-line programs—anti-dialogical they may be—represents the utter failure of our institutional models of social work education.

III

HUMAN SOCIETY, SOCIAL CONSTRUCTS
AND INTERVENTIONS

"You must be the change that you wish to see in
the world."

M. K. Gandhi

Key Constructs

Social Transformation • Social Work: Education,
Practice and Research •Social Intervention.• Social
Practice • Social Policy • Social Praxis • Social Welfare
and • Social Contract

The construction of social reality is a phenomenal abstraction
that impinges upon human and social behaviors in varied
manifestations. Our responses and patterns of cultural reactions
institutionalize this continual strife in linear and multilinear manner.
Both individual and society follow an evolutionary trajectory until
a cataclysmic change occurs due to social, political and cultural or
natural upheaval of historic proportions.

A revolution is, by definition, a radical intervention that
consciously and subconsciously helps erupt an inescapable lava of
change. Its outcome is both unpredictable and challenging. Social
transformation may and may not be a byproduct of revolution. What
recent history suggests is that revolution itself is in an evolutionary

phase. From Bolshevik Revolution to the Arabian Spring, we witness varied uprisings with unreliably different outcomes. Since *change* is the constant with universal validity, I have ventured to explore this reality in different contexts.

When I became a student of Social Work in 1958, I had envisioned a professional intervention to be the Holy Grail of desired social intervention. In principle, my innate belief still holds water. What did not transpire is the 'self-fulfilling prophecy' as revolutions devour their own children. Even the forces of the Enlightenment did not bring about the Age of Reason. I have hypothesized that much of our social malaise is because of the demise of our primordial Social Contract. I have pleaded for the Enlightenment II to see that a new social contract does insure a better world devoid of ignorance, poverty and violence. Ideally, ***the goal of social work is the end of itself.***

Social Work involves a whole nexus which I call Education, Practice and Research (Mohan, 1988). This *SW-EPR* is an interdependent system with complex disciplinarities. Some local and regional zealots of "practice" have politically criminalized "teaching" and "research" if they are not governmentally *credentialized*. Sure, brain surgeons, plumber and barbers require proper credentials. However, certification of the professoriate should not be left to clerically appointed boards whose members behave like vindictive bounty hunters with impunity. Practitioners' anxieties will not be resolved by 'killing mocking birds'; they must strive hard to become knowledgeable judges beyond their juvenile impulses.

Essence and Ethos: Citations

"The main burden . . . is to demystify the cult of a practice that lacks validity and authenticity. Social work's ontology is posited on the balance of certain mandates: distributive justice, quality of life and optimum freedom [for all]. We have not yet reached our Jordan. We remain a hopelessly fragmented group uncommitted to our mission: social equality, justice and freedom."

UoSW: RSR (1999: xi)

"Contemporary social work is a mirror rather than candle."

UoSW: RSR (1999: xv)

"The progress that social work has made as a profession is both impressive and remarkable. Yet, I feel genuinely concerned about certain aspects of the professional culture that I find worrisome for the future of our profession. *A new fundamentalism seems to eclipse our rational faculties that are otherwise conducive to secular theodicicy.*"

UoSW: RSR, (1999: xvi; *emphasis added*)

"The Parsonian system and its 'mandate of social agencies' and emphasis on "client"-centered "practice" is untransformational at best (Gouldner, 1971). Clientization is not a humanistic approach. Also, to emphasize 'micro' at the expense of its "macro" dimension and their symbiosis is an intellectual impossibility."[14]

"Ever since the abstraction of *social contract* came into reality, intellectuals across nations have debated the duality of government versus free market. A society without regulations amount to a jungle. Fiscal fundamentalists have however conveniently asked for a law of jungle in the markets while commanding an authoritarian hand over other aspects of law and order. This paradoxical double-behavior has caused a situation which calls for a revolution, i.e. *social contract II* (Mohan, 2007) .... Societies have collapsed and civilizations have

---

[14]   Brij Mohan (2012): Humanistic social work: core principles in practice, by Malcolm Payne, Journal of Comparative Social Welfare, 28:1, 85-86; http://dx.doi.org/10.1080/17486831.2012.636260 (Feb. 28, 2012).

fallen when people have refused to learn from history. When the history of our future is written, one would be tempted to allude to one or all of these elements at the roots of the contemporary crisis of development.

1. The fall of the Berlin Wall
2. Theocratic fundamentalism
3. Nine-Eleven
4. Globalization
5. Iraquification
6. The rise of the other (Mohan, 2008b ; Zakaria (2008)."

DPoC&SP (2011: 34-35)

"It's hegemonic snobbery to propound an iron law for others. In a fast changing world still mired in age old trappings of human-societal conflicts, we are condemned to relive a past unless we read, understand and follow the lessons of history. The future of social development, in other words, depends on how we as individuals and communities reach and treat each other. It's imperative that social development's iron law will be etched in the foundation of a civil society which stands on the twin pillars of global equality and social justice (Mohan, 1988)."

DPoC&SP (2011: 39)

"Intervention is not a new invention. Humans have devised varied modes to intervene in crisis and pre-crisis situations since antiquity. *Social intervention,* a post-war construct employed by therapeutically oriented professionals and policy practitioners, seeks to preempt and eradicate dangerous situations that thwart human and social development."

DPoC&SP (2011: 121)

Pre-and-post-crisis intervention poses difficult challenges for professional practitioners and researchers who should clearly understand three principles of social intervention underling the art and science of positive change:

1. Understanding dialectics of human behavior is important to design any therapeutic/transformative intervention;

2. Acceptance of a renewed social contract and its implications for desired social change; and,

3. Modeling appropriate social interventions beyond textual prescriptions and territorial imperatives."

DPoC&SP (2011: 123)

"The new global conflict—post ideological nihilism—is essentially a meltdown of the existing social contract."

DPoC&SP (2011: 145)

"Social Work as a profession is a 20th century American innovation. Its evolution is a mark of the rise of the Welfare State. These states of welfare institutionalized residual functions and ensured people security against the contingencies of modernity. The 21st century realities are starkly daunting and different. We notice meltdowns in our basic social, economic, and political institutions. The troubled manifestations of these cultural crises are beyond the SW-EPR purview, competencies and even imagination. The 'rest of the world' is emulating the American model, which is inherently dated. This is internationalizing a flawed model of education, which is so vitally important in a newly global world. A truly *postmodern* approach to problem solving implies radical changes in program and curricular structures, pedagogies, epistemologies of change."

Journal of Social Work Education, 2011, 47.3: 621.

"The organization of social work theory, practice as a field, method and process is largely the outcome of the Western sociological "imagination" embedded in the systems theory. My research in the field suggests that the organization of social welfare system and its functions are primarily guided by Parsonian theory of action, which we don't teach at all these days. I am no fan of Parsons' macro-functionalism; yet, silver-plating an old vessel with postmodernist polish is no justice to either theory and/or practice ([DPoC&SP]) Mohan 2011)".

Journal of Social Work Education (2011, 47.3: 622)

"'Obsolescence of social work' is premised on the notion that 'person in social environment'—the object—has become obsolescent [in reality] . . . The dissociation of human and social realities is an outcome of professional politics. A sense of rediscovery is essential to achieve a synthesis . . . . Unification, universalization, and demythologization of knowledge, values, fields, and methods are necessary processes to regenerate social work's vitality, identity, and legitimacy".

EoF (1993: 108; 110)

"Profession X has a chameleon character. As a parasite, this creature has thrived on a unilateral relationship amongst its cognate disciplines. [This] academic parasitism of social work has cost this discipline its own identity. Paradigms of research, human behavior, social policy, and practice have generated a chaotic confluence of interdisciplinarity that lacks both substance and validity."

UoSW: RST (1999: 8-9)

"Anthropocentrism has had a corrupting influence on the development of human psyche. One of the fundamental issues in the history of science has been consciousness construction leading to human freedom. Human emancipation , however, is a continuous saga. . . . Empirical objectivity is modernity's greatest myth. . . . Social workers are people who have studied and learnt the art and science of caring. This professional endeavor involves a litany of roles, and goals, and strategies as conceptualized by the skilled pioneers in the field."

UoSW: RST (1999: 14-15)

"As an academic specialty, [social work] remains a second class citizen in the community of established disciplines without any rigorous efforts to assert its identity. Its 'otherness' thus emanates from a cultural neurosis that sustains inherent contradictions. Liberatory concatenation [free of] ideological fissures and epistemic resistance is bound to generate a fuller view of social reality denied so far by an incomplete profession."

UoSW: RST (1999: 20)

"The unification of knowledge is not only a scientific mandate ; it also is humanistic perspective. If social work fails to acknowledge and implement this imperative as a mandate, future generations of social workers will continue to strive for their identity and mission. I seriously doubt if we have been able to invent our future; our continued dependence on others is a sign of our self-deserved devolution."[15]

UoSW: RST (1999:20; *emphasis added)*

---

[15] There is nothing more descriptive of this reality than the cascade submergence of social work schools with other departmental units with some unanswered questions. Our acquiescence to administrative fiat is a confession of our feckless status. I call this devolution.

"Globalization of economy, democracy, and science is changing the patterns of relationships, specialties, communications, and institutional designs . . . . There are encouraging signs of secularization and progress; there is unsettling evidence of professional archaism, rational ossification, and ideological regression. The result is less transparent , more bureaucratic social world that is unwilling to recognize the structure of new evils: obsolete curricular designs; unscientific research models; self-serving leadership; antidialogical settings; crassness of careerism, and a nearly cannibalistic pursuit of success."

UoSW:RST (1999: 30)

"Social work's epistemological foundations are based on academic parasitism, unreflective view of social reality, and uncritical self-awareness . . . . It is common experience that social work faculty and students abhor deeper discussions on philosophical-critical issues. Without exaggeration, the social work culture is expediently anti-intellectual."

UoSW:RST (1999: 32)

"While most American social workers contend with private practice with the victims of sexual, spousal and substance abuse, realities within national boundaries and beyond call for a radical transformation of purpose and method of the profession itself. The inability to seize this challenge amounts to the end of social work, as we knew. The awareness, however, calls for a new social work."

UoSW:RST (1999: 33)

"Social work has become a faith-based calling in its own perverse style: Vagina Dialogues preach reverse discrimination; scholars write more texts than they read; administrators wallow in unabashed self-promotion; and careerism flourishes at the expense of professionalism. In short, academic social work has become practitioners' haven for faith-based theodicy that is neither committed to knowledge-building nor philosophically sound pedagogy. In the name of scientific research, we have become apes of unfounded empirical logic which lacks both authenticity and legitimacy."

RSW: RMSP (2005: 9)

"Social work is not what we occupationally pursue as careerists; social work is what we do professionally and personally to change this world . . . . Seven pillars of radical self-renewal are postulated here as the foundation of new social practice. . . . A holistic philosophy of thought and action generates osmosis of hope. Social Work as conceptualized and practiced is an anti-intellectual construct. . . . The poverty of our literature and its devolvement is a monumental collective failure [of] our self-description. In The Logic of Social Welfare (1988), I ventured to suggest Social Praxeology . . . . [As] I have grown, I submit Social Practice."

RSW: RMSP (2005:177-78)

"Ideally social work should be seen as a human-rights profession . . . . Social work, a quintessentially human rights approach to most of the human-made tragedies, may well reequip itself, both pragmatically and epistemologically, if its smorgasbord is focussed on universal, indivisible, and inalienable areas of the evolving structure of human rights."

FvD: CH&SD (2007: 100-101)

"A new social work detours through a century-old benign inanity towards a proactive holistic goal involving seven intertwined steps of self-renewal. Horizontally, in a time and space continuum, these elements may be conceptualized as a matrix along different dimensions including (1) culture; (2) value and values; (3) ideology and faith; (4) science and technology; (5) governance and organization; (6) education; and (7) social relationships (Mohan, 2005)"

FoD: CH&SD (2007: 139)

"The new kind of social work will rise as a phoenix form the ashes of an obsolete client-centered theology. . . . Theory and practice of social work warrant emphasis on inclusive citizenship, universal equality, freedom and justice. What we need is practice of hope rather than politics of expedience."

FoD: CH&SD (2007: 139-140)

"We as a professional community face a threefold challenge:
1. Examine the mission of social work in light of main scientific advancements;
2. Analyze the impact of objective and subjective interpretations of social reality on theory and practice; and
3. Critique the success and failure of professional culture in light of the challenges of the twenty-first century."

FoD: CH&SD (2007: 169)

"Social policy is viewed here as societal response to historico-political injustices that have been inflicted on humanity in the name of dogmas a free society cannot accept. Now that the 'darkest' century is behind us, we must embark upon a new age of innovative directions with hope for a better world."

Journal of Policy Practice (2011, 10, 2: 95)

"Policy innovations, by intent and definition, are progressive directions toward change—social change that ameliorates poverty and heals the wounds of an unjust feudal, colonial, and imperial past. Globalization, after all, failed to be the patina of cross-national democracies.

There would be no need for any policy innovation if human society were an impeccable system. Since we live in a less than perfect world, intellectuals, especially policy thinkers and practitioners, must reflect on and build upon individual and collective experiences that will insure a better world for our posterity."

Journal of Policy Practice (2011, 10, 2: 96)

"India's advancements aside, its entropic public corruption, a primitive bureaucracy and nearly chaotic politics must be good news to its nemesis . . . . India's 4000 km long borders with two hostile neighbors in cahoots with each other cannot expect Gandhian passivity from India while they themselves pursue aggressive policies. China's one party government offers coercive social policy framework, which is a contradiction in terms. Social policy is quintessentially a democratic response to societal needs. But democratic freedom, like India's, is a monstrosity that muffles any hope for constructive development."

Journal of Policy Practice (2011, 10, 2: 98)

"Social policy must be conceptualized as a liberating mechanism directed toward social justice."

(*EoF*, 1993: 116)

"Social policy is a creative decision-making process that involves a complex system of cognitive offshoots and politico-social-economic variables undergirding a unified whole of transcendental values and technoscientific advancements. Policy making is a tough value-oriented balancing of probabilities rather than hunt for convenient possibilities.

"Yet, policy quintessentially is a science and art of the possible. Social policy ought to be conceptualized as a possible theory and practice of the preferred societal values, goals and interventions. The range of social policy includes: alternatives that economize resources and optimize human function without oppression, allocations that generate creative mechanism without ugly political maneuvers, and strategies that promote conducive social arrangements without counterproductive results."

NHSW&P (1985b: 5-6)

"If the roots of social policy lie in the social contract thesis, the determinants of human behavior ought to be explored in an evolutionary framework. The concept of interpersonal human behavior, beyond the Judeo-Christian-Moslem conformity and Freudo-Marxist determinism, has come of age: ward of anxiety and preserve self-esteem."

NHSW&P (1985b: *133*)

"[There] is a new horizon for policy analysts and theorists. The world realities of contemporary cultures and political systems dictate that each nation move to a progressive direction to become a dynamic whole of the universe. Our unconsciousness of this reality will amount to a self-destructive illusion"

NHSW&P (1985b: 134)

"Since human behavior, social welfare, social progress, scientific developments and global wellbeing cannot be—in fact, should not be—dealt with in culturally isolated pockets, comparative analysis [becomes] a viable means for ***unification*** of fragmented theories and approaches that concern universal wellbeing."

TCSW (1985a: 3)

"A decolonized society with an aversion to
progressive social change, rampant with political
corruption, becomes a fertile field for the mushroom
growth of divisive and disruptive forces . . . . While stress,
restlessness, anxiety and insecurity grow in general,
disparity between haves and have-nots and the gap
between principles and practices internally decompose
the entire system."

(*ISP,* 1972: 106-07)

Conclusion

Society is an abstraction; human society is a construction
which requires consistent and careful reconstrcution. Social
transformation does not occur in an evoluationary process; it takes
consciousness and deconstrcution to bring about changes that
are crucial for remaining human in an otherwise adhoc system.
Social interventions ought to design and implement mechanisms
of change that maintain human equllibrum without oppressive
hierarchies. We would not seek any social policy (and welfare) if
human society were in perfect harmony with our avowed goals.
All we need is a peaceful coexistence that promotes humankind's
wellbeing.

IV

INTERNATIONAL ASPECTS AND ISSUES

"If madness is the truth of knowledge, it is because
knowledge is absurd, and instead of addressing itself to
the great book experience, loses its way in the dust of
books and in idle debate; learning becomes madness
through the very excess of false learning . . . . In a general
way, then, madness is not linked to the world and its
subterranean forms, but rather to man, to his weakness,
dreams, and illusions."

Michel Foucault (1965: 25-26)[16]

New Internationalism • International Society •
International and Comparative Social Welfare • New
Social Development • Human Rights • Globalization •
South Asia • World Peace and Coexistence

International social development is a post-war guilt and
delusion; it represents the western quest for new inroads into the
existence of the so-called developing nations. The *Third World* thus
became a home and asylum of the world's wildest madmen, women
and children. Poverty, illiteracy, backwardness and violence marked
them off the civilized world. They must be saved form themselves;
else, civilization would perish! This gospel has been the rationale for

---

[16]   Madness and Civilization: A History of Insanity in the Age of Reason.
Trans. Richard Howard. New York: Vintage Books, 1965.

crusades, invasions, and inquisitions. More recently, master plans echoed these "mantras of mayhem" to recycle the ruins of colonial destruction. Much of international social work is an attempt to export global fantasies of an ill-defined profession.

The notion of 'universal family' (*Vasudhaivakutambhkum*) existed long before the dawn of modern civilization. Societies fraught with territorial imperatives and fissures of self-interests, are glued together with certain myths of invincibility. Modern nationalities remain barbarously primitive when it comes to reason with a neighbor. Israel and Palestine, India and Pakistan, Tibet and China, North and South Koreas and, lately, North and South Sudan are excellent examples where the fires of hell have been alight ever since divisive occupation and partition came to existence.

Since I have a cross-national upbringing and trans-national education and experience, the cause and rationale for internationalizing social work has been dear to me. I have envisioned even the construct of an International Society. I published the findings of my first research on mental health in *International Social Work* and *Mental Health Digest* (US Department of HE&W) before I came to the United States. However, in this land of freedom, I have seldom seen a field as narrow as "US-Based" Social Work[17]. The Council on Social Work Education's continued endorsement of such an exclusionary view is unfortunate[18].

About twenty-five years ago, Ramesh Mishra and I talked about writing something on social welfare with a global framework. Since we both are solo writers, we published our books on the subjects independently but with mutual respect. *Global Development: Post-Material Values and Social Praxis* (Mohan, 1992) grew out of a paper that I presented in Lima, Peru at the 25th International Congress of Schools of Social Work (August 15-20, 1990). The subtitle of the

---

[17]   *Cf.* A concept paper by Richard Estes on ISW at CSWE's website.

[18]   *See* Munn, Jean C. Teaching Note—Viewing the world view: Visual inquiry in international settings, *Journal of Social Work Education*, 48.1 Winter 2012:167-177.

book was the main burden of my paper, which, to my utter surprise, received an overwhelming response in Latin America. Again, when I visited Brazil and Chile two decades later I received similar responses. This convinced me that "US-Based" approach is fundamentally hegemonic[19] and fraught with individual-institutional narcissism[20]. There is no room for such trappings in a noble profession like ours. The continued politics of exclusions are counterproductive at best.

Essence and Ethos: Citations

> *"Poverty of Culture* (PoC), as a theoretical formulation, assumes significance for three reasons: 1) The awesome effect that Culture of Poverty (CoP) has had on social policy and programs; 2) its misleading and often flawed assumptions and implications; and 3) its alliance with the forces of reactionary violence against every liberal cause."
>
> *DPoC&SP* (2011: 9)

> *A society which thrives on its neurotic trappings that sustain inequality, insecurity and inhumanity in various forms of cultural stratifications and patterns is essentially a predatory system that incubates the Poverty of Culture (PoC).* A simple schema depicts its dynamic of design and structure:

A. Institutional Predation (*stability* vs. chaos)
B. Axiological Inequality (*morality* vs. anarchy)

---

[19] *See* Sonia Kapur's review of *Trans-national social work practice* Eds. Nalini J. Negi and Rich Furman (New York, Columbia University Press, 2010) in Journal of Comparative Social Welfare, 27, 3, 2011: 270.

[20] Conscious exclusion of a superior work with arrogance borders on conceptual apartheid. Only an insecure person would do so. The truth of the matter will unravel when the history of ISW is rewritten in the spirit of objective inquiry.

C. Cognitive Arrogance (*knowledge* vs. ignorance)

"These structural elements are based on both rational (conscious) and irrational (unconsciousness . . .) motivations."

DPoc&SP (2011: 11)

"Humanity's survival depends on its need to perpetuate as a species. This goal is hard to accomplish unless societies unlearn self-destructive behaviors. The daunting challenge that all scientists and intellectuals face today is to devise a strategy of global transformation which involves borderless progress and enduring peace and development. The myth and reality of this formulation involves critical analysis of issues and forces beyond the kitsch of developmental delusions."

DPoC&SP (2011: 25)

"The main promise [underlying this delusion] is to demystify the nature of contemporary social development that is, from a global perspective, is dysfunctional at best. This formulation is postulated on three assumptions: 1) human and social development is symbiotic both functionally and structurally; 2) our systems of knowledge, governance and cultural patterns suggest multi-linearity of approaches; and 3) peaceful development is a myth unless we universally humanize these systems and approaches."

DPoc&SP (2011: 26)

"The *development delusion* in a globalized culture is a fascinating subject for informed debate and discussion . . . . The author offers a hermeneutical system of linkages that seeks to connect certain dots out of the box. The kitsch of developmentalism lacks legitimacy, coherence and relevance in a "flattening" complex world. From nation-building to globalization, dualities of triumphs and tribulations mark a neoglobal order that breeds 'de-developmentality' of chaos. If September 11 ominously heralded the end of an open society, the hegemonic Iraq quagmire represents a perfect storm."

DPoC&SP (2011: 26-27)

"Contemporary International Social Work tends to *spatialize* its objects of study. Since humankind's well being is intrinsically linked with science and social transformation, the vocabularies of change merit meaningful contextualization (p. 131) .... In a world so radically transformed by the forces of new Keynesianism, fundamentalism, and self-serving internationalism, we must pause and rethink the problems, issues and possibilities that lie ahead of a viable specialty that we call International Social Work (ISW)."

DPoC&SP (2011: 131-132)

"An internationally accepted definition of social work is not necessarily International Social Work (ISW). When organizational committees and task forces assume a defining role they often lose contact with stark reality. Pieties of organizational mandates and self-fulfilling prophecies reinforce a tautology of ineffectual approach to lofty ideals. Unfortunately, ISW has become a victim of this fallacious advancement."

DPoC&SP (2011: 132)

"International Social Work (ISW) may be defined as a discursive discipline that employs the knowledge and tenets of social practice in a diverse, dynamic and interdependent world. In reality, it is more of a field rather than discipline. ISW's ethics and methodology are designed by the contours of social reality that represent human life as an end (in itself) in an otherwise divided world."

DPoC&SP (2011: 133; emphasis original)

I postulate seven basic formulations which may be useful in theory construction in the field of International Social Work.

1. In a hopelessly divided world, "the flattening" theory (Friedman, 2005) does not adequately explain: Apocalyptic dissolutions marked by Terrorism, AIDS, Poverty, Refugees, Ethnic Cleansing (Darfur) even the response to our own Katrina catastrophe! Yet, each of these constitutes "international" problems.

2. "Interlocking" and "Person-in-social environment" (PIN) perspectives help unravel but don't constitute a social work theory *per se*.

3. "Intersubjectivity" and "interpretive" hermeneutics are crucial elements to theorize human behavior with "sincerity" rather than reason. One must, however, remember philosopher Harry G. Frankfurt's dictum[21].

4. Social work's "objectivity" is a conceptual delusion; the true measure of any "objective" social practice lies in its effectiveness in short and long term resolutions.

5. "Internationalizing" in the context implies: acceptance of a dynamic world, which is "flat" (globalizing), combustive, in the throes of many conflicts; and challenging: (because of) poverty, genocide, AIDS, inequality, authoritarianism, fundamentalism, terrorism and lack of understanding and tolerance.

6. The failure to recognize that social problems have increasingly become "international" amounts to intellectual *bad faith*. When knowledge and

---

[21] "Our natures are, indeed, elusively insubstantial—notoriously less stable and less inherent than the natures of other things. And insofar as this is the case, sincerity itself is bullshit." (Frankfurt, 2005: 67).

technology become the causes of problem, one must surmise and re-think: Do we have a correct theory? Remember, arrogance is a greater source of misfortunes than ignorance.

7. Comparative-analytic approach to study international issues is a step toward scientific exploration. "Our science is not knowledge (*epitémé*): it can never claim to have attained truth, or even substitute for it, such as probability" (Popper, 1968: 278).

DPoC&SP (2011: 136-137)

"The new challenges that social work and social development . . . communities face may broadly be grouped in three categories: 1) Cultural-ideological; 2) professional and intra-professional; and 3) global. Category wise, these challenges may further be broken down into 3 sub-categories evolving as a conceptual framework for future discussion and study.

Social Work's Post-Ideological Challenges: An Aesthetico-Global Framework

1. **Cultural-Ideological Barriers**
   a) Theorize (causality, scientificity with an open but critical mind)
   b) Conceptualize (new constructs and models of theory and practice)
   c) Analyze (facts, values and ideologies)
2. **Professional and Intra-professional Strains**
   a) Legitimacy
   b) Identity and authenticity
   c) Inter-disciplinarity
3. **Global Issues**
   a) Universalize (knowledge)
   b) Contextualize (problems, policies and programs)

c)   Empathize and actualize ("Think globally and act critically" (Mohan, 1997)

While it may not be possible to escape the full blown effect of social climate, it is imperative that professional values and ethical standards are not compromised."

DPoC&SP (2011: 151-152)

"New Social Development (NSD) is conceptualized as a post-material process of human-societal transformation that seeks to build identities of people, communities and nations. As a field and strategy of social reconstruction it employs different models and modalities of *social practice* that suit varied situational-ideological imperatives in a given environment. By and large, two models characterized by centralized and decentralized location of power represent a spectrum of developmental process."

DPoC&SP (2011: 159)

"The perils of progress seem to imperil the future of Social Development as we would like to see. Sartre famously said: Success is not progress . . . . The kitsch of 'developmentalism' lacks legitimacy and relevance in a "flattening" world. From 'nation-building' to globalization there are harsh dualities in a complex neo-global order that breed certain 'de-developmentality'. The idea of *New Social Development* signifies the symbiosis of human and social development as a mega project of global-social transformation. The foundation of progress, it may be argued, is rooted in the conviviality of a post-ideological coexistence. This implies that a second Enlightenment is an imperative of our future. A new epoch that promotes counter-hegemonic analyses, policies and programs at the expense of age-old myths is in order."

DPoC&SP (2011: 165)

"A theory of new social development is essentially a counter-hegemonic argument; it's premised on the notion of human emancipation that is conducive to i) peaceful coexistence ii) in a world without terror iii) signifying diversity of peoples in an international society based on equality and justice. The stated goal, in light of world realities, appears utopian at best, foolhardy naiveté at worst. But, I am not alone in this journey to the center of truth."

DPoC&SP (2011: 41)

"It's not wars, guns and votes that militate against developing democracies as experts like Paul Collier would have you believe (Collier 2009). It's cultural meltdowns of varied hues that destabilize systems of sustenance which render democracies vulnerable to the creatureliness of reptilian behaviors."

DPoC&SP (2011: 58)

"In general, we are left with three important lessons [about the Politics of Development]:
1. A new policy pendulum that swings along human trappings independent of market forces;
2. Volatility of social contract and its implications for international peace and *nation building*; and,
3. Need for post-colonial social interventions beyond ideological prescriptions and territorial imperatives."

DPoC&SP (2011: 59)

"The Enlightenment *paradox* has transformed epistemic ethos into bureaucratized disciplinarities. As a consequence, specialization of knowledge unwittingly breeds anti-intellectualism since both epistemic discourse and discursive formations are subverted by arrogance and ignorance."

FoD: CHSD (2007: 3)

"The ordeal of human-and-social development is fraught with conflicts and contradictions in the fog of post-ideological chaos and territorial-cultural wars. Scenarios of sound social action, coherent policies and nurturing progress are seldom found."

FoD: CHSD (2007: 4)

"The possibility of a reflexive-positivity, apparently a contradiction in terms, is a formulation that posits the object-subject duality in an anti-essentialist, post-modern context. It enables examination of contemporary life events, behaviors and their patterns in a context that accounts for discontinuities of existent knowledge."

FoD: CHSD (2007: 8)

"As a civilization we have failed to eradicate world poverty and violence. While there is evidence that world conflicts have declined after the demise of cold war, it is uncertain if our sense of security has substantially risen to a comfortable level. On both macro and micro levels, one finds a disturbing pattern of dissonance and disconnection."

FoD: CHSD (2007: 9)

"The notion of a biodiverse universe must be postulated in terns of diversity that promotes equality and justice among all members of the human family . . . . Any development that does not comply with metavalues of a free and diverse world is bound to be counterproductive."

FoD: CHSD (2007:22-23)

"**The Body and Soul of Development**: A few observations are spelled out here toward a developmental matrix of ethical transformation that nourishes humanity without destroying its ecosystem:

1. Sublimate techno-feudalism in the interest of humankind's general welfare;

2. Regulate hyper-commercialism and corporate rapaciousness in the service of societal goals ; and

3. Liberate humanity from its own anthropocentric hubris."

FoD: CHSD (2007: 24-25)

"The contemporary development and progress is both a parable and parody of our paradoxical present: An unpalatable sandwich of an abhorring past and unconquerable future. Human nature, history, and geopolitics account for the continuing crisis of modernity. To save us from ourselves, we need a common commitment to the survival and dignity of the human race."

FoD: CHSD (2007: 38)

"The new ethics of Social Development is committed to recognize the Bill of Rights of all children to live in dignity without the pain and disgrace of this existential reality."

FoD: CHSD (2007: 39)

"Contemporary social devlopmentalism is fraught with the fallacies of growth. In a world plagued by paroxysm of neuroses, fear, self-righteous contempt, violence and global inequalities, universal needs—survival, justice, and human dignity—call for new strategies for social transformation."

FoD: CHSD (2007: 77)

"The motifs of social development are flawed in conception and design. Social development, as an isolated national plank of policy and planning, is doomed to failure as its vacuous disconnectedness from the human drama of events and socio-political realities is intrinsically counterproductive."

FoD: CH&SD (2007: 79)

"Denial of human rights—a universal and pervasive evil—is the genesis of all social exclusions. The matrix of social exclusions involves a complex array of cultural, economic, political, religious and ethnic injustices that are practiced on various levels in different degrees. Social hierarchies as they become functional—caste and slavery, for example—serve as the incubators of social exclusions."

FoD: CH&SD (2007: 84)

"We live in a new age of heightened neurosis marked by fear, contempt and self-righteousness. New Social Development [NSD] as a strategic perspective must aspire for an inclusive society that is founded on the principles of coexistence. Universal human needs warrant global solutions.This premise, however, is untenable unless (1) terrorism and war, (2) inequality and poverty, (3) abuse of human dignity are declared as the true 'axes of evil.'"

FoD: CH&SD (2007: 84)

"Once human rights are universalized and implemented , a new culture of work, production and distribution will evolve where 'global human needs' will warrant alternatives far better than personalized saving accounts. As a fulcrum of human decency, rights-based reality will eliminate the need and significance of assets-and-faith-based reality."

FoD: CH&SD (2007: 87)

"Thus a new Social Contract II is in order to facilitate *NSD* after 9/11, Rwanda, Darfur, and Guantanamo Bay."

FoD: CH&SD (2007: 88)

"If I were to define my strategy to achieve the best of 'globalization,' I would unhesitatingly say: *Internationalize the American Dream.*"

FoD: CH&SD (2007: 91)

"Human rights are conceptualized as inalienable rights of all peoples required for the survival, security, and dignity of each individual, group, and community without prejudice or discrimination . . . . Are we truly citizens of a free world?"

FoD: CH&SD (2007: 92)

"We need a new social development that would universalize the basic tenets of universal justice and human rights. A *universal model of human-social development* is an imperative for promoting minimally acceptable human conditions . . . *We have achieved an unfree word in a hopelessly ill-defined culture of freedom.*"

"Globalization, unless wedded to fundamental democratization, appears to be a false messiah . . . . It is also within our reach to dream of a world without poverty and war. But, we as scientists, policy makers, gatekeepers and 'believers' of our respective faiths have failed humanity to insure a better world for the future generations."

FoD: CH&SD (2007: 102)

"Internationalism is premised on a global consciousness which can be both hegemonic as well as egalitarian. . . . Social development must be compatible with progress. Acquisition and progress are not analogous concepts. (p. 88) Globalization of market economy, privatization of human services, and individualization of social needs seem to thwart the possibility of a sustainable culture. A nexus of forces calls into question the validity and efficacy of social development as a method. A diverse and pluralistic world is being torn apart by the ravages of ethnic, sectarian and neoimperialist violence (p. 90) . . . . Democratization and social development are interdependent processes . . . Developmental perspective is fraught with issues that concern three areas of major concern: (1) Third Worldization of development; (2) globalization of conflict; and (3) new worldization of order (p. 94).

EoF (1993: 88-94)

"Economic nationalism, ethnocentric militarism, xenophobia, and world capitalism are bound **to create multipolar superpowers** embedded with corporate rapaciousness. The impact of this neoglobal climate is unlikely to change to foster peace and justice in the world community. Social development and its life-sustaining thrusts can serve two functions: it can be an 'alibi' for perpetuating the post-industrial perversity; it can also become a casualty of the post-industrial society. In either instance, social development as a world project shared by all national communities as a universally accepted model of global welfare is unlikely to emerge a "bioglobal" paradigm (Mohan, 1988) of hope and dignified coexistence."

EoF (1993: 95-96; emphasis added[22])

---

[22] Cf. Fareed Zakaria's, *The Post-American World* (NY: W.W. Norton &Co., 2008) published fifteen years after the publication of *Eclipse of Freedom* (Mohan, 1993).

"Comparative social welfare seeks to analyze attributive variables of welfare systems across the board: it attempts to unravel human conditions, policies, institutions, values. Resources, methodologies and delivery systems of various societies, portraying differential dimensions of and approaches to complex social issues and problems."

TCSW (1985a: 1)

"Comparative welfare, by its definition and nature, cannot be a value-free endeavor since varied societal conditions and arrangements are studied within a framework that is built upon humanistic, universal and transcendental values. If social misery, for example, is the focus of a comparative study, it implies a critical-evaluative approach to the analysis of historico-societal forces (feudalism, colonialism, imperialism, fascism, etc.,) that have caused global ill fare."

TCSW (1985a: 12)

"The method of comparing is perhaps the oldest human endeavor that led to empirical and experimental inquiry. We compare and judge; evaluate and assess; distinguish and validate—all in the process of authenticity that rejects and accepts certain assumptions and concepts leading to theories and generalization. Basic assumptions underlying this framework are threefold:

Human commonalities, despite vast differences, constitute a system of unity that may be called universal humanity.

Mutual understanding and awareness is a positive strategy for establishing endurable relations with interacting others (groups, societies, and nations).

An intelligent and sincere assessment of the world situation (forces, conditions, and relations) suggest that global welfare is prerequisite to cross-national harmony and order."

TCSW (1985a: 4)[23]

"International social work, especially with emphasis on comparative methodology, is a human response to unravelling differential social issues, problems and approaches. Enhancement of the human condition—beyond territorial, ideological, and socio-cultural barriers—is a global challenge. Scourges of governmentality perpetuating global oppression negate the essence of freedom that all people are entitled to enjoy. Social welfare offers no panacea; it represents a consciousness against cross-national dehumanization that thwarts global welfare."

GoI&CSW (1989: ix)

Conclusion

National boundaries and societal territoriality represent the evolution of civil society. Which is why we have law and order to prevent disputes and resolve conflicts that arise from perpetual avarice and discord. New internationalism is premised on the notion of an international society that would eschew human destructiveness and

---

[23] These basic, underlying assumptions of 'comparative social welfare,' constitute the structure of a 'comparative-analytic' framework that has inspired many a formulation but without due acknowledgment. Comparative Social Welfare's misfortune has been that it's neither well understood nor duly appreciated by those who need it most. It's my belief, CSW must be included in the Foundational Courses of all master's and doctoral level offerings in social sciences in general, social work, welfare and policy in particular. CSW is a valid, viable and crucial method and perspective in international social work. It's unfortunate "US-based" ISW conveniently remains no- cognizant of its own origins.

pretentious develeopmentalism. I am painfully aware of the limits of benign hope. *Global Development,* as I see (1992), is a collective challenge for all nations and regions. International Social Work, the way we propound and proffer in the West, is a feckless and delusional endeavor without much essence and substance.

V

THE SCIENCE, VALUES AND SOCIAL REALITY

"It is a Faustian science, and within the limitations of life on earth it could propose to do great things. It is Kantian science, and a Deweyan one: it is bounded by man's limitations, and it is dependent on man's active transactions with its environment. It doesn't take over the full task of religion since anthropodicy is not a theodicy: it would limit itself to the use of human powers effecting whatever they can to overcome avoidable evil. Man would abandon otherworldly groupings for unrealistic ideals, and content to make his meanings unfold in the material, everyday world."

Ernest Becker (1968: 376)[24]

---

[24] Becker, Ernest. 1968. The Structure of Evil: An Essay on the Unification of the Science of man. New York: The Free Press. I quote this passage from one of the best books written during the last fifty years in social sciences. Unfortunately, Becker did not get the recognition he deserved.

Key Concepts:

Unification of Science • Humanistic Positivism •
Ideology and Dystopia • Democracy •Culture • Chaos•
Evil • Poverty of Culture

C. Wright Mills was right: Science is a pretentious messiah.
Like a sharp knife in a surgeon's or thug's hands, it can perform two
opposite functions. Hence functionality, for lack of a better word, is a
cautious imperative to license any scientific advancement. However,
functionality is not a value-free concept. We invaded Iraq based on lies
in the name of democracy. Pakistan prides itself on its nukes designed
and directed to destroy India's major centers of development. China's
robust capitalism dwarfs any western rapaciousness.

The conflict between values and science is nor a new one.
Objectivity, truth and general wellbeing have been the cornerstones
of universal morality, if there is such a concept. In this century, after
the horrors of its immediate predecessor, it assumes great importance
to synthesize science and values. This partakes of special significance
in a globalized world, which seeks to globalize democratic values
and practices.

Both Science and technology do not exist is a non-societal
context. Societal wombs generate fears, delusions and hope. Great
civilizations have disappeared—or *Collapsed!* —when disasters
threatened extinction. Are we headed toward such a cataclysmic
end? Perhaps not. The book of Revelation was written by a spiritual
pornographer. I believe in science and its cause. Science is man's
greatest weapon against dogmatic heresies, which have brought
nightmares and mass murders. It's incumbent on intellectuals of the
world to see that fight against unreason and inhumanity is not lost.
Neither science nor reason will safeguard it. There is no dearth of
great scientists and rationalists.

Humanity calls for enlightened citizenry to impact the shape and
outcome of democratic processes that guide our destinies. Education
is one such vehicle if properly harnessed and brilliantly imparted.
Another 'heretical' pronouncement is that of annihilation of despair

all around the globe, not just in the darkness of developing nations. Should policy makers, public leaders, and corporate executives conveniently forget these basic mandates, it's not the bloodthirstiness of Revelation that will annihilate all of us; it will be the madness of one Dr. Strangelove who will preside over a common destiny of total doom. This is not a Biblical prophecy; this is a rational conclusion of an ordinary humanist who can think globally and act critically despite the clouds of culturally inclement weather. Jonathan Turley comments that western nations have begun 'criminalizing free speech."[25] As if the demise of dissent was not enough. "Where governments once punished to achieve obedience, they now punish to achieve tolerance. As free speech recedes in the West, it is [now] silence that is following in its wake" (Turley, 2012).

Essence and Ethos: Citations

> "The idea of *Poverty of Culture* (POC) is thus proffered as a unifying theme for unraveling the dynamics of inequality and injustice and corresponding interventions and policies that have either failed or become counterproductive . . . . PoC is offered as an argument against the prevailing orthodoxies and practices that partake in social sciences [and] dysfunctionally impact human and social development processes. The poor, marginalized, underprivileged peoples in the Global South present serious challenges to the credibility of globalization in the post-American World. I take issues with current *develeopmentalism* and its social aphasia."
>
> *DPoC&SP* (2011: xiv-xv)

> "If the twentieth century was the age of revolutions, the twenty-first century will be remembered as a

---

[25] http://www.latimes.com/news/opinion/commentary/la-oe-turley-criminalizing-speech-20120309,0,3460649.story (March 9, 2012).

post-revolutionary era when absolutes of ideology melted away in the heat of global dynamics. The bumpy road ahead is not a hindrance; it is a challenge that we have to accept professionally and truthfully."

Journal of Policy Practice, 2011, 10, 2: 96

"The burden of post-ideological policy agenda should: a) *de-Platonize,* b) *humanize,* and c) *contextualize* policy innovations as the main goal of social transformation. A search for society that is free from violence, terror and dehumanization is a continuous process. Delusional it may seem it's a paradoxical outcome of a dystopian culture that we have accepted as a bargain for unprincipled success and consumerist survival. The fundamental values of a civil society that we all seek to achieve are compromised in the process of what we call social development. The point is: social-human development should be interdependent; public and social policies ought to be congruent in this process; and world governments should strive for peaceful coexistence in the common interest of international decency, dignity and survival."

Journal of Policy Practice, 2011, 10, 2: 99

"There is no cure for ill-diagnosed mass dementia that is often consumed with individualism, hedonism, communism and capitalism."

International Review of Modern Sociology (2009, 35, 2, 259-270)

"The ontology of knowledge is ridden with paradigmatic vicissitudes that obscure the symbiosis of truth and existence. A crisis of consciousness unleashed by the paradoxical forces of the Enlightenment continues to mystify the methods and ethos of scientific inquiry."

UoSW:RST (1999: 42)

"Theory and practice, mind and body, facts and values, and the empirical and the apriori constitute varied contexts in which we posit the structures of knowledge in relation to social reality . . . . Scientism, despite its unitarian emphasis, failed to achieve universal freedom. Somewhere in this itinerary of a supposedly lofty process, intellectuals forgot their mandated role in the very society they live in and seek to serve. The angels of reason became inadvertent victims of unfounded faith. As a result of this self-imposed myopic vision, goal-displacement has gradually transformed a benign servant into a monstrous reality that has eclipsed both reason and freedom."

UoSW:RST (1999: 42-43)

"The human condition, social reality, and scientific progress logically constitute a valid framework for legitimizing the authenticity of knowledge if pursuit of truth is the ultimate scientific goal. In light of this postulate, the failure and success of modernity ought to be examined as a universal project."

UoSW:RST (1999: 45)

"If scientific progress had followed the ethics of development in harmony with universal values, the dawn of the twenty-first century should have been pregnant with equality and justice across nations. Instead, we have a world ravaged by horrors of new tribalism."[26]

UoSW:RST (1999: 46; emphasis added)

---

[26] The prescience of this statement by a new flash as I write :http://www.economist.com/node/21548233?fsrc=nlw%7Chig%7C2-23-2012%7Ceditors_highlights (February 23, 2012)

"Objectified knowledge, hermeneutic interpretations, patterns of changes through cumulation, relativistic and positivistic outcomes are products of different organization . . . . The praxis of philosophy, in the post-Nietzschean vein, deconstructs metaphysics aesthetically heralding the new mythology of Dionysus, the absent god who is coming for discourse. This Nietzschean counter-Enlightenment culture of thought—the end of philosophy—is perhaps the crux of the scientific paradox."

UoSW:RST (1999: 47-48)

"Authenticity of communication and purpose of knowledge , then, must decide the context and character of scientific norms and practices. Social praxis undergirds the essence of progressive social theory and practice . . . . Demystification of postmodernity's alienated consciousness on the one hand and revival of the Enlightenment sense of values on the other, constitute the theme of a mega project which all scientists must join to achieve universal freedom. **This is the essence of unification.**"

UoSW:RST (1999: 51-53; emphasis added)

"Objectivity, humility, and practice constitute three elements in a philosophical design that seeks to relate the abstract to the real. This implies a synergy not yet seen in social sciences. The lack of imagination is perhaps the continuing problem. In our 'search' for objectivity, we have been wallowing in the empty hall of knowledge without intuition and imagination. This quest has been corrupted by our sibling jealousy that feverishly impels us to mimic the style and method of hard (natural) sciences."

RSW: RMSP (2005: 6)

"Post-ideological nihilism defines the nature of modern evil and contemporary dystopia. The end of history, however, was not meant to be nihilist. The culture of death, fear and insecurity has become a universal reality."

FoD: CoH&SD (2007: 44)

"The contours and character of evil are both complex and chameleon . . . . Social-psychological theoretical spectrum posits evil in a variegated instinctual-institutional context mystifying inexplicable human behaviors . . . . The nexus of evil encompasses a range of individual and institutional patterns (of carnivorous nature) that involve both predatory and defensive behaviors. The evolution of this formulation is grounded in the history and anthropology of human-social development. The Neolithic hunters and food gatherers were not predators; they became corrupt, violent and rapacious when they began to settle down as owners of private property. In other words, the rise of a cvil society heralded demise of Rousseauean "primitive innocence."

FoD: CoH&SD (2007: 45-47)

"If evil is innate, both benignity and malignancy tend to be products of the quality of social transformation that changed the primitive society for better or worse. In other words, the evolution of the 'anthropological Adam' is a consequence of phylogenesis that transformed human society."

FoD: CoH&SD (2007: 47)

"Between Shakespeare and Checkhov, Shakespearean tragedy, it seems, is deeper, than the latter's. I hope I am deadly wrong. It sum, cultural decadence, political corruption, and surfeit of religious bigotry have nourished a ghoulish culture of death that breeds fanatic intolerance, pathological hatred and political terrorism . . . . Unless nations, societies and cultures of the world rebuild a new culture, chaos will prevail and pessimists will win against all notions of civility and order."

FoD: CoH&SD (2007: 63)

"Science is an amoral creature. Its venom can be life saving and therapeutic yet deadly at the same time . . . . Application of a rational-humane design in search of a window on an otherwise dark horizon is a plausible and prudential conjecture . . . . The idea of Logical Humanism thus emanates from a retro-modern despair of post-modernity . . . . It is 'logical' to end the hubris of modernity's triumph and to strive for a world which is livable. This benign pursuit of survival with humility and hope is endlessly sustainable."

FoD: CoH&SD (2007: 157)

"Fallacies of Development warrants a working symbiosis of human and social development, abridging a long-standing hiatus between the human and social."

FoD: CoH&SD (2007: 176)

Conclusion:

If science were a messiah, society would have been a paradise. Alas, this did not happen. Despite the Enlightenment, technological advancements could not escape ideological trappings of a deeply troubled civilization.

Man remains incomplete and lonely in a crowded world of seven billion social animals. The rise of 1%—99% divide marks modernity's greatest misfortune. It's not sciences' fault that majority of the people are poor. It's however some one's fault that brought down the established societal institutions. Cultural, fiscal and political meltdowns are byproducts of irrational hubris. Poverty, honestly, is not an economic problem. It has been, and will always remain, a political issue unless we synergize scientific and cultural advancements toward achieving a just and decent future. It's not the culture of poverty, it's the poverty of culture that breeds the most dangerous twins, ignorance and arrogance.

FOR THE RECORD:
10 QUESTIONS FOR BRIJ MOHAN[27]

Kirpal S. Soodan and Usha R. Srivastava[28]
Lucknow University

1. What is your vision of Social Work in the 21ˢᵗ century?
The 21-century social work has to be a different than what it has been in the 20th one. In a fast changing world professions that can't adapt will perish. Social work is a very popular profession, however. Social Work's future, as I envision, is rather uncertain unless we demythologize our approaches quite radically.

2. Why did you leave India?
This is a question that has dogged me since I left India March 1, 1975. It's the "push and pull" reality that reached its climax for me in the early seventies: Lucknow University was engulfed —literally and

---

[27] Reproduced with publisher's permission (originally published in *Journal of Comparative Social Welfare*, 2010, 26, 1&2: 281-285). The author is most grateful to Drs. Kirpal Singh Soodan and Usha Rani Srivastava, Lucknow University, and Michelle Whittaker, Permissions Department , T& F Journals, for allowing the use of this section question.

[28] Drs. Kirpal Singh Soodan and Usha R. Srivastava, Department of Social Work, Lucknow University, Lucknow, 226007 India. This conversation was initiated by the two contributors in December 2008 when Dr. Brij Mohan visited his alma mater, Lucknow University, to deliver a keynote address to an International Conference. JCSW is grateful to both for putting Brij on the "spot" for the benefit of posterity and his own work. Editor, P. D. Allen

metaphorically—in the fires of political and social turmoil. When Canning College was set afire by the hired hoodlums of Gopal Tripathi, erstwhile Vice Chancellor, Lucknow University Teachers' Association (LUTA) assigned me to edit and publish *Save Lucknow University* (1973). Between LU and LSU, my journey has been rather smooth and stable despite many ups and downs. L.U. taught me the ropes in addition to giving me an identity; LSU has sustained me and my work in a foreign land and I am grateful to both.

3. You have been called "Sartre of Social Work". Can you explain this comparison for general consumption? In India you are known as the "Father of Indian social psychiatry." What is your most important work?

I am both flattered and embarrassed with such comparisons. I would rather be known as Brij Mohan of my own discipline. But my discipline has no definite identity. Hence, at times I feel an intellectual orphan and a gipsy. This is no disrespect to Sartre whose philosophy did influence me in 1960s and beyond. His life and work have been my major inspiration as a thinker and writer.

I think that my Ph.D. dissertation still stands out as a seminal contribution. Last year I was invited by the Int'l *Association of Social Psychiatry* to give a paper in Istanbul and I was happy to see that Social Psychiatry is still alive and well somewhere. My investigation of the human condition within classic mental hospitals revealed a lot more than I was looking for. Madness is far more common and complex than normally understood. It's the *banality of madness*, if you will, that I find more intriguing and challenging[29]. As such, much of what flowed out of my consciousness deals with human dignity (freedom), oppression (alienation) and its dialectic (dialog).

---

[29]   We discussed this issue with Dr Mohan at length. He contends—and it's hard to argue with him on this one—that madness and civilization cannot be separated (in his Foucaultian vein).

4. Have you accomplished what you had aspired to achieve in your post-dean years?

Yes. And, no! I resigned from the administrative position to invest myself completely to the academic life. Being a former dean is the most unenviable job in academia especially if one stays too long at the same place. During the last 23 post-dean years at LSU, I have published a dozen books, firmly established a new doctoral program and an international journal, and taught innumerable courses, not to mention about 200 conference papers, articles, reviews and chapters. This has been a stunning success in spite of less than ideal conditions. What I could not achieve is a sense of fulfillment. There has always been a Sisyphean challenge. I am embarrassed by the duality of my success and failures, you can say.

5. You have written extensively about the crisis of social work. What is your present take on this issue?

Crisis of Social Work exists in one's mind. To me, its credibility issue has long been a source of stress and challenge. When I became Dean of the LSU School of Social Work (1981), our School was a 2nd class citizen in the academic community. Relentlessly, I pursued the goal of establishing a knowledge-based doctoral program. This entailed transformation of the mission, which enraged people who were not committed to sound scholarly accomplishments. The situation has not changed much, substantially. If it has, it has gone from bad to worst. Our profession is still talking about "competency-based" learning; asset-based policy and social work research has not gone beyond dated interventive models that lack scientific validity. Above all, derelict leadership and unabashed careerism has been a disappointing development. It's not "professional imperialism" as some populists contend; it's institutional-individual narcissism at the expense of innovation, ingenuity and inquiry that breeds mendacity and mediocrity. We are all prisoners in Plato's Cave; I had the audacity to throw off my "chains". The blinding Sun outside taught me how to see reality. I try to go back to the Cave with some hope but I find myself totally alienated. It is not the Cave that bothers me anymore; it's the rise of the new *Panopticon* that I find very unsettling. There is an urgent need for transformative knowledge. Nothing is more perversely hypocritical than chanting the mantras of diversity and practicing nefarious "isms" at the same time. I have survived many a pernicious motif of exclusions; now that I turned 70, *ageism* appears to be insurmountable. In India, seniority and age is traditionally respected, recognized and rewarded. In the US, it's neo-Darwinism at it best.

6. Do you have a theory of social work?

No, I don't; nor do I believe in a theory that would validate social work education, practice and research (SW-EPR) as a unified whole. I do have a theory of social transformation that calls for *unification of social work.*

7. Since you are a product of Indo-American education, how do you signify your work in your newly adopted country in an increasingly diverse and "global" community? Conversely, how is your New Social Development theory relevant to the Third World conditions where exploitation of children from India's sweat shops to Africa's tribal wars is so hideously prevalent?

It's the LU-LSU symbiosis that has shaped my thought and practice. I have tried my best to connect both in a transparent manner. One can see through my work what I stand for. I think India gave me a body with a soul that I have been able to develop in the process of acquisition and dissemination of knowledge in my continued pursuits for an inclusive global civil society. I have pleaded for *international citizenship.* There has to be a new way to rethink our existence on this planet. Time is almost running out.

Exploitation of the powerless, in all demographic groups, is an international tragedy. In India, domestic servitude is a national disgrace. I haven't seen a place where young children are not employed in menial jobs. Sexual predation and economic servitude of women and children is inescapable outcome of a predatory culture where certain rotten traditions and rapacious systems perpetuate. *New Social Development* (NSD) rests on the premise that societal evils—poverty and racism for example—are oppressive outcomes of pervasive inequality and injustice. As I have said, it's not the *culture of poverty*; it's the *poverty of culture* which is at the root. It's a civilizational challenge to overcome this atavistic impulse. I am not an optimist in this respect, however.

8. You have written about social work as "the other profession." Can you elaborate this notion?

As I said, this refers to the legitimacy issue. It's not merely social work's inanity; it's *irrelevance* that mocks its mission. There is dissent amongst the Iranian clerics; but there are no voices (of dissent) in academia today. Social work, organizationally, is not a very open system; our textbook culture, adherence to evaluative standards, hierachized educational relationships and deification and demonization (of selected people) simply go against the spirit of academic freedom. Just compare NASW's *Encyclopedia*—controlled exclusivity by a few Schools and manufactured for the desired outcomes, not knowledge—with the Wikipedia revolution.

9. In the Preface to your Fallacies of Development (2007), a very eminent theorist, Christian Aspalter, alludes to your theory of human freedom and oppression, which precedes Amartya Sen's views on freedom and social development. Could you elaborate this interface?

In 1984 I was hospitalized for a major abdominal surgery. During my agonizing painful post-operation recovery, I gave notes to my wife and vaguely constructed a theoretical framework, which we both presented a few months later at the Montreal Symposium IUCSD. Later on I also published this piece as an introductory chapter to *Toward Comparative Social Welfare* (1986). My thesis is that human oppression and freedom constitute a dialectical whole; individual-societal freedom depends on *our* choices— people, policies, and programs—that determine the quality of life. If this formulation is empirically validated, one could easily think of a matrix as global paradigm. Amrtya Sen is a very influential Nobel Prize-winning economist which I am not. But note what stupendously arrogant Economists have done to our economy and society. Most of my ego-ideals never won any Academy Awards; one even refused a Noble! My work stands on its own merit. *Success* is not my forte. I have lived a Sartrean dictum: *success is not progress.*

10. What are your most favorite books, movies and places? Give at least 3 names. Any plans to retire?

There are three books that I love to read again and again: *Words* (Sartre), *The Birth of a Tragedy* (Nietzsche), and *The Structure of Evil* (Becker). I love many movies. My most favorite movies are *Devdas* (Bimal Roy's), *Pyassa, To Kill a Mocking Bird,* ` *Lawrence of Arabia* and *Godfather.* The places that I like most include Paris, New York, Lucknow, Hong Kong, Santa Barbara and Los Angeles.

No, I don't have a definite retirement plan yet. I am at the peak of my professional experiences and I enjoy my work more than ever. Yet, I am conscious of the ominous eventuality. The so-called "stereotype threat" for want of any credible reinforcements has indeed been a concern. But I have always found the ultimate joy in the essence of my work which continues.

POSTSCRIPT[30]

1. In India you are still known as 'the Father of Social Psychiatry". How has this background helped your professional status in the US?

Your doctoral research goes a long way to define your professional identity and destiny. I am no exception. My Indo-American odyssey, however, greatly impacted this transformation. The mental health industry here has become a racket. No wonder madness is our most lucrative export. Unfortunately, it took a heavy tall on my sensibilities and development. But I had learned early how to use adversity to my advantage. This dictated opportunity helped me expand my intellectual horizons and which in turn enriched my own education. Not many people in my profession have understood let alone use Sartre, Nietzsche, Habermas and Foucault on the one hand and Buddha, Kabir and Gandhi on the contrary. In fact there seem intuitive-occult undercurrents that tie and synthesize our thoughts. For example, even though Foucault remained unknown to me until mid eighties, I always saw India's caste system as its cultural Alcatraz, a prison system that no one escapes. This is equally true of my research in mental hospitals. I had not known about Foucaultian thoughts on 'madness' as a doctoral student but I was into 'insanity' beyond the institutional walls of 'asylums.' On a recent sabbatical (2005), I revisited those institutions in Agra to Bangalore. My convictions and views about mental health practices and policies remain unchanged. Too bad, in the US, I was never allowed to teach, let alone practice, mental illness

---

[30] These seven questions were added by the initial interviewers who have co-edited this books. I gladly accepted the suggestion as it befits the context in closing.

and therapy. The DSM cult overrides rationality. By default, I became a policy and development oriented social philosopher. I hope I have answered your question.

2. **The last we met and talked, you categorically denied about your plans to retire. Suddenly, you did it! What transpired that changed your mind?**

Honestly, 'retirement' is a euphemism; I resigned (in protest) since I could not withstand the toxicity of a less than tolerable working environment. The chemistry of budgetary politics and ageism—which supersedes all other 'isms'—is almost lethal. Survival without dignity is dehumanization. May we, please, move on to your next question?

3. **There is a sense of crisis in academia. How does it impact higher education in general and social work in particular?**

Academics face daunting challenges in a fast changing world. Can't you see, the most brilliant and successful achievers of this era—from Steve Jobs and Bill Gates to Mark Zuckerman—have been college drop outs? The campus crisis is invisible in the labyrinths of its hidden corruption, structural anachronism and a near czarist CEO leadership model. A capricious system of recognition, reward and endowments cannot promote intellectual freedom. It incubates mendacity and arrogance with impunity. No wonder academic programs are increasingly less valued compared to administrative, athletic and other non-curricular endeavors. As a result, one of our most democratic institutions has become a hideously top-down hierarchized system. Social work, in my view and experience, is a microcosm of the general rot. Others will survive—you can't substitute mathematics, chemistry or history for that matter!—but disciplines like social work, journalism and their ilk will atrophy in due evolutionary process. Since social work's goal is entirely different than other disciplinarities, we must stop mimicking others. Where as altruism and problem-solving processes will always remain within social science domain, social work has failed to demonstrate its effectiveness and relevance in a complexly evolving global society. The citadels of its 'institutional-individual power' may well have succeeded in their narrow missions; a new cult of mediocre punditry, 'diversity' politics, and vocational orthodoxy—antithesis of my "practice of hope"—is certainly owed to them.

I have already written too much on the subject. Social work does not need me any more. Perhaps it never did. My adolescent idealism of late fifties and early sixties, and again, the challenges of Post-Reagan years, forced me to look at social reality from a *rational-humane* perspective. The ideological pendulum does not stop; it goes on. Careerism in social work promotes feckless agents of an illusive change. Our confluence of cluttered clichés of 'empowerment' cannot change the *status quo*. As a belated realist, I have come to know the limitations of my calling. But at the end of the day, I have a great feeling that I was privileged to serve academia all my life. Teaching, I believe, is the best (and the least corrupt) profession. It's no accident that incompetent teachers successfully achieve higher administrative positions. Also, *credentializing* bodies that seek to *clientize* social work pedagogy by inquisition behave like cartels of illegitimate power. This exclusionary culture poisons the very ethos of our freedom and democratic values. Academic acquiescence which cannot protect and nourish these fundamentals betray the very essence of inquiry and research.

Universities in general enjoy the status of cognitive fiefdoms; there is a premium on its membership. While students need them for survival, faculty and administrators many times use their privileged positions to advance their careers and bank balances. This contradiction amounts to a revivalism that bodes well for predatory instincts. Much of research, especially in fields like social work, journalism, and education is an outcome of funded grants that helps university coffers and bolsters summer salaries for incompetent anti-intellectual professionals (I wrote most of my books in financially arid summer vacations while our administrators went on paid vacations). The unfortunate consequence of such practices is the growth of incestuous scholarship where the fruits of students' work are enjoyed by their supervisors with impunity. Sadly, university system nurtures these trappings in the name of collaborative, funded research at the expense of independent scholars. This would explain, partly, my near immobility, vertical and horizontal, during quarter of a century (1986-to date).

4. What are your post-retirement priorities? Is an Autobiography in the works?

I have been working on things—keynote lectures, conference papers, lectures, editing, publishing and advising—that I enjoy most. Many reputed universities sustain senior faculty on ridiculously fabulous salaries. I am modestly happy what I do here as an LSU pensioner. What matters is your work.

Currently, as you well know, I am working on My Omnibus—and thanks for helping me out!—which will be released soon by i-Universe, USA. My next project, and perhaps the last, is a debut novella, The *Death of an Elephant*, which excites me most. I began working on it long time back but it's only now that I could complete. I have already revised it seven times. I am still unsure if it's ready to go to the press. Papa Hemingway always inspires me when it comes to writing. But I am no Hemingway. I will be lucky if I could get a publisher. It has been a galling task to write fiction since I am not trained as a novelist. Now I have become a full time writer, which I always wanted to be. Thanks to my retirement! I am still ambivalent to do my autobiography. But a few close friends whom I respect, have persuaded me to do so. I am in the process of negotiations with a publisher to write, tentatively entitled, this book as *Truth Matters: Conflicts, Convictions, and Confessions of an American Dean*.

5. What does the 'death of an elephant' signify? Can you elaborate on the substance of your novel? What's it all about? What has inspired you to go to fiction now that you are known as a social philosopher all over the world?

The 'elephant's death' I refer to is based on a true-life experience from my childhood. The poor creature was poisoned to death by his own care-taker. To me Ramu (pseudonym for the victim) embodies, allegorically, the inadvertent protagonist's role to signify the end of innocence. The novel in general is about *nothingness* by which I mean 'absence of unfreedom.' There is no suspense or thrill; nor is it meant to be a moneymaking, compensatory detour from the duality of my career. Cathartically, I have stitched together many an otherwise insignificant recollection as a reality-based fictional quilt. A good fiction is actually a better representation of reality since one can enjoy literary license to speak out truth, fearlessly, that cannot be told in a hopelessly libelous, sometimes vindictive, culture.

On the whole, I am not a pessimist that I appear to be. There will be a moral equivalent of the Arabian Spring in academia as well. It will sanitize the temples of learning against the contradictions and hypocrisies of a hierarchized system. I have faith in our students; they never failed me. Regretfully, I cannot say the same about my generation (of educators).

Most social work administrators are paid poseurs equipped with self-interests unlike their students and faculty who are usually trapped in benignity of success without seldom questioning the rationale for status quo. The problem arises when *individual-institutional narcissism* overrides ethical obligations inherent in our calling. If social work, education, practice and research stand for social justice and freedom, we must eschew narrow and nefarious objectives. In part, this anomaly is compounded by general organizational goal-displacement. If you stand for what you believe in and work at the dictates of your conscience, you may not not even survive, let alone succeed. I have lived through an extended professional ordeal marked by subtly ostracized exclusions, abominable discrimination and open hostility punctuated by occasional symbolism of hollow grace; it has been Kafkaesque. Let me hasten to add, it's not the university as an institution; it's the evilness (of rivals and charlatans) and their banality that is usually at the root of every reprehensible exclusion. Since most of our universities serve on the classic dictum—which is absurdly mythical—that 'a dean can do no wrong!"— it is well neigh impossible for any one to find recourse against institutional authoritarianism. I tried once in 1988; my attorney almost sold me out to the university's power. In a university town where football is the *religion*, one should not expect any fair deal unless you are locally well connected. This was also true in Lucknow and its fabulous university but the legal system there, despite its imperfections, was always open to university faculty and students. In US it's nearly unthinkable to file a law suite against a university administrator, let alone win it. The 'holy cow' status will not last for ever. That's a sign of hope.

6, 7. Finally, two more questions. How is this 'US-based' model of social work helpful to internationalize our profession when 'indegenization' has become a norm in the so-called developing nations? As we find in South and South East Asia, countries are retooling their concepts and methods which hardly bear any "professional" character. Second, isn't 'developmental/transformational social work' a contradictions in terms? How are we going to address regional imbalances when social inequality, economic crisis, and international conflicts are adversely affecting global development? Last, finally, what's your most favorite quote?

Kirpal and Usha, you guys ask tough questions. To avoid simplistic explanations, I would like to quote from a Letter to the Editor, *Journal of Social Work Education* (1989, 45.1 Winter, 151) that I wrote on some of the issues that bother you both after half a century of dedicated service. To paraphrase a joke by poet-comedian Surrender Sharma, "Our true dreams are not those that we visualize in night; the ones that keep us sleepless are the real dreams." Having survived the pain of decades of anguished Ambien dreams, I have come to realize the limits and strengths of my profession. I will be less than honest if I did not acknowledge this fact. The excerpted Letter that I quote below will answer the crux of problem:

"A Dialogue on Social Justice (Editorial, JSWE, 44.2 Spring/Summer 2008: 1-7) is a valid vantage [point] to take stock of our professional purpose, culture and future directions. 'The future of social justice is the future of social work' I wrote sometimes back (Mohan, 2002). . . . The call for social justice has become rhetoric at best and hypocrisy at worst. This state of professional evolution is a malpractice and we, the educators, leaders and organizations like CSWE and NASW, are implicated in this intellectual fraud. Sonia Hawkins (a pseudonym) lately resigned from an MSW program chiefly on account of our 'cultish' methods and practices that a therapeutic society imposes on 'captive' often naïve but genuinely concerned students. So long as social work remains a microcosmic mirror, it cannot serve as a candle (Mohan, 2005)".

As regards your last question, Usha, I think there is a total disconnect between rhetoric and practice. Essence without ethos is righteous *BS;* ethos without essence is shallow self-piety. Social Transformation has lately become the sexiest theme, next to Empowerment. The truth is not many people understand what it means, let alone how to achieve and comprehend its implications. University administrators care about their own jobs, careers, and budgetary issues which a team of MBAs would handle much better. Faculty and students are locked into a new kind of Faustian bargain characterized by the consequences of an eternal cobra-mongoose conflict. Communities at large treat these hallowed institutions as temples which they are not. This may sound cynical but elements of inconvenient truths are seldom known to public. It's from those depths of despair that your voice rises like a phoenix. Sartre said it best:

"Life begins on the other side of despair"

Afterword: On the Banality of Madness

"Capitalist industrial society (like the 'socialist' state-capitalist societies) is profoundly irreligious . . . God and Mammon: to each his own. This compromise and the illusions it produces may be effective for a long time, but man awakens always awakens again, notices that he is merely dreaming, and demands salvation. Only a changed reality, a society that realizes the principles of love and human autonomy throughout its structure, can satisfy this demand."

Erich Fromm (1982:294-295)

Man[31] is a lonely creature, incomplete at best, predatory at worst[32]. Human anxieties and anguish resonate cultural upheavals and civil malaise. We have just gone through meltdowns from the Wall Street to the Main Street. The outcome is a disturbing sense of unrecognized helplessness. Disillusionment and angst can be sources of uplift; what we experience today is a numbness of conscience and paralysis of will that endanger full human-social development (Mohan 2007; 2011).

We are at the cusp of a *third industrial revolution*[33], *which* is about to *totalize* technologies of production, quality of life, social reality and

---

[31] I shall use this expression in a generic sense—as an anthropologist would—without any gender bias.

[32] This piece is based on my Keynote Address delivered to the International Psychological Applications Conference and Trends 2012, May 24-26, 2012, Lisbon, Portugal

[33] *The Economist* (Cover), April 21-27, 2012: 3-20.

relationships. Still an eschatological confusion envelops our cosmic existence in a norm-less "wilderness". [34]

We remain free in a very unfree world. This existential paradox defines the nature of contemporary madness, which involves mass murder, terror and war as metaphors for unbridled freedom and monstrous liberty.

"On all sides madness fascinates man." (Foucault, 1965/1988: 14) My fascination transcends spatio-temporal boundaries as I seek to draw your attention to some of the most hideous human manifestations that are no where even in the new, due out shortly, edition of DSM V (*See* Cloud, 2012).

I am not talking about the complexity of any "Criminal Minds" or the monstrosity of an Evil Empire. The burden of my paper is to reflect on the banality of a new atavism that thwarts all civilized endeavors to coexist in peace and prosperity as a human family.

Our civilization is built on the mountains of human skulls of unknown martyrs and unsung heroes who were crushed, conquered and buried under the debris of local and regional kingdoms. De Gaulle once said: "cemetery is full of all famous people." A true history of the survival and triumph of human spirit is not yet written. Britain has recently destroyed records of its colonial crimes [35]. In such a world culture, innocent and powerless individuals and groups have remained—and continue to languish—in the Darwinian jungles of avarice, anxiety and arrogance (Mohan, 1993).

---

[34] Vance Packard (1968) would not be surprised how close his analyses came to reality.

[35] Britain destroyed historical records of its colonial crimes. See http://www.guardian.co.uk/uk/2012/apr/18/britain-destroyed-records-colonial-crimes (April 18, 2012)

But, Herbert Marcuse, summed it up best: "Man is free even in the hand of his executioner." (Marcuse, 1970)[36]

Notions of 'totality' and 'madness' date back to hoary antiquity. However, post-war monstrosities simply morphed these otherwise benign concepts into a totalitarian terror that permeates our subconsciousness. Totalization is not 'totality'.

My approach to the subject is critically reflective[37]. I submit an *assemblage* of my thoughts about human and social reality that belies easy explanation from any *plateau* of organized ideological vantage point. Before Daniel Bell declared the death of ideology, Deleuz and Guattari had refuted its very existence: "There is no ideology and never has been"(1987: 4). End of ideology, however, should not be misconstrued as 'end of history'. Ideology is—and has always been—a euphemism for conceptual-territorial triumphal wars.

I would like to "problematize" a noology *of praxis*, which involves a call for ethical society and corresponding reflective-representational social development[38]. An inherently violent culture with gladiator fetishism cannot incubate sustainable peace and prosperity, let alone promote human development. "Madness of mass murder"[39] is not

---

[36] "Here, to overcome the repressive features integral to Freud's concept of sublimation, Marcuse turns to Nietzsche, conceptualizing a form of sublimation as activity that escapes the Logos of domination to become part of the Logos of gratification." Cf. C. Holman, 'New German Critique,'http://ngc.dukejournals.org/content/39/1_115/67.abstract (May 5, 2012).

[37] Sartrean-Neitzschean (inclusive of Freudian-Marxian) on the one hand and Gandhian on the other.

[38] I humbly reject all contemporary kitsch of social development that is force-fed to young students in the name economic and social uplift of the so-called 'developing nation.' See, Mohan, B. (2007; 2011).

[39] This has a reference to President Barak Obama's recent comments on the continuing crisis in Syria.

confined to a particular region or religion; its ubiquity is writ large on the collective psyche of global power.

The ambiguities of the rise and fall of democracy are both intriguing and complex. Seventeenth century and later, the Enlightenment consciousness devoured the King; Nietzsche announced: "God is dead." However, scientific advancements, innovations and technology eclipsed 20th century as the "darkest" phase in human history. Indeed the Twenty First century inherited a mixed baggage. No wonder we can see the ominous signs of 'darkness at noon' even at the helm of our success.

Platonic philosophy and its essentialist offshoots—"universal" truth, universal perfection and "justice"—have successfully sustained the established order. Global economies and the rise of new class of elites have mostly enriched and empowered organizations and people on the top. Hence we have massive, pervasive alienation. The forces of oppression and consequential circumstances have reinforced new hegemonies of power and control that are fundamentally flawed and undemocratic. Capitalist 'freedom' has seen its Waterloo puzzling "Red Princelings" of The Chinese Century[40]; [41] (*see* also 'The Great Fall of China' (Coy, Roberts and Einhorn, 2012: 6-8).

We are passing through a contrapuntal-paradoxical era beyond the known Dickensian dualities. We are increasingly alone in the most wired—may I say weird?—world. The nightmares of Cold War have gone but the fears of Cyber Wars are frightening. Indeed 'war' has become a communicative lingua of day-to-day disagreements

---

[40]   *See* Hannah Beech (2012).

[41]   "The South Korean government revealed Monday that it recently seized thousands of capsules filled with the powdered flesh of dead babies. Reportedly, some people believe the powder has medicinal purposes and was created in northeastern China." (http://news. yahoo.com/blogs/sideshow/south-korea-seizes-capsules-containing-powdered-flesh-dead-190306280.html May 7, 2012)

and conflicts. From "dog war" to "mummy war," our presidential debates are full of nonsensical skirmishes, which do not belong to any civil society. On a larger reality plane, Star War fetish permeates our existential reality from the Pentagon to Quince's[42] playroom, which looks like a museum of Star War legos. Commercialism has invaded the child's world with pernicious and perpetual need for the last toy that does not exist[43]. ***"Obsolence of man"*** (Marcuse, 1970: 44; *see*, also 1969; Mohan, 1993: 108-109) ***has destroyed the innocence of child***[44].

There are veritable signs of incredible economic growth in the world's poorest countries (China, India, and Brazil; lately, Turkey and Indonesia); equally bewildering is a of new inequality scale, 1% vs. 99%, in the world's richest country. A nearly anarchic Wall Street culture and its economic fall out shook the whole world but business as usual persists in the corridors of power. Bernard Madoff and Lehman Brothers basically shattered the myth of marketplace secularism. These anomalies are both dystopian and Shakespearean in their meaning and impact.

Ascendance of global democracy has grotesquely emerged with a rising tsunami of general inequality: 1% vs. 99% dichotomy is no more an American tragedy. While India launches Agni V, an

---

[42] Quince is my three-year-old grandson with an amazing sense of good heartedness. Like all other grand parents, I love to "spoil" him and his 6-year-old brother Aneel. But the problem is culturally deeper than space allows me to elaborate here.

[43] My point is: This maddening toy race is destroying a child's initial inclination for attachment and belongingness. No psychologist or sociologist has addressed this issue in a convincingly constructive manner.

[44] There is an element of truth in Rousseauean concept of "primitive innocence."

intercontinental missile[45], nearly 1 billion of its teeming millions still live in stark poverty. American social scientists have thrived on the myth of a "culture of poverty" that has sustained a politically volatile, socially dysfunctional, economically indefensible and psychologically alienating system of *welfare* that has become a dirty word in the civilized world.

Poverty is not an economic problem: it's basically a political issue, which an ethical society can only ill-afford to ignore (Mohan 2011). Individual freedom and mental health policies, like wise, are not exactly 'psychiatry' issues. What we confront today is a conundrum of a schizophrenic society. If society were an individual, DSM would come handy to label him/her as "crazy." No one recognizes the fact that DSM itself is a product of an insane society, which manufactures war, alienation, and hollywoodized scripts of "wellness". *The Politics of Therapy* is no more a 'dirty' secret of the mental health industry (Halleck, 1971; *see* Szasz, 1970). The *myth of mental illness* (Szasz, 1974) has become an aspect of *poverty of culture* (Mohan, 2011).

Indeed wellness and healing is our top export. "The globalization of American Psyche" (Watters, 2010) is more of an indictment than diagnostic critique. Mental Health professions, social work included, should demythologize the myth of madness.

As certitude and sophisticated applications make life easier, ubiquitous skepticism and uncertainties have become the hallmark of our contemporary crises, which manifest themselves at all levels including social and natural, local and global, normative and empirical.

Having made these prefatory observations, I would like to emphasize three dimensions of human-developmental crisis: 1) Totalization (for dignity, social justice and universal equality); 2) Unification

---

[45] http://news.yahoo.com/india-tests-nuke-capable-missile-able-hit-china-034308390.html (April 19, 2012)

(in knowledge, science and practice); and 3) Demystification (of positivist utopian delusion).

A theoretical model may be formulated to underscore the symbiotic linkages that unravel the complexity of our conundrums, conflicts and challenges.

Exhibit 1
Totalizing Human Reality

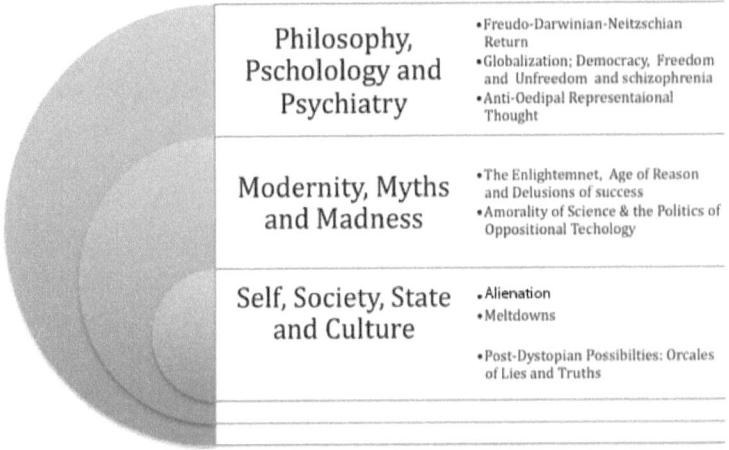

Philosophy, Pschology and Psychiatry	• Freudo-Darwinian-Neitzschian Return • Globalization; Democracy, Freedom and Unfreedom and schizophrenia • Anti-Oedipal Representaional Thought
Modernity, Myths and Madness	• The Enlightemnet, Age of Reason and Delusions of success • Amorality of Science & the Politics of Oppositional Techology
Self, Society, State and Culture	• Alienation • Meltdowns • Post-Dystopian Possibilties: Orcales of Lies and Truths

In light of these formulations depicted in Exhibit 1, I venture to hazard a few a priori assumptions that help formulate a logically humane basis for further discussion.

1. Dualities of existential reality are false and misleading;
2. Social and human development *is* inseparable; and,
3. Progress, not success, is a road to social transformation.

This triune of human-social development sketched above is a continual process of social transformation and each culture invents its own path for self-renewal. The normative-structural designs, which are not always conducive to human dignity, are outcomes of this transformative system.

However, behavioral morality is a product of this process. There is a trend to "medicalize" morality, implying genetics as the determinant of human behavior[46]. This intellectual heresy based on the politics of religion seeks to "totalize" psyche with far reaching and unknown consequences.

The role of science, technology and education in the ideological state is *tantalization* of the human condition. Dialectically this trend has backfired on the states of welfare as well as oppression. Disintegration of colonial empires, the former USSR, and other contemporary authoritarian regimes is suggestive of challenges that lay ahead on the road to freedom, justice and peace. The fall of Berlin Wall heralded the rise of *the others*. Yet true freedom remains a distant dream for 99% of the human race inclusive of western democracies[47].

I would hazard three main observations with humility and skepticism about the role of ideology, reason, and state that seem to thwart human dignity in search for freedom.

---

[46]   *See* Jonathan Haidt's *The Righteous Mind* (2012).

[47]   The 'end of ideology' is not the end of its mythologies. A kind of meltdown permeates cultural landscapes. From Tea Party movement to Wall Street Occupation, one finds the general discontent of people against which they have no power. According to a Pew Research report:
"The inequalities have risen to historically unprecedented heights. In the words of the report: "The Occupy Wall Street movement no longer occupies Wall Street, but the issue of class conflict has captured a growing share of the national consciousness." (April 30, 2012)

Exhibit 2
Fragmentation of Human-Social Reality

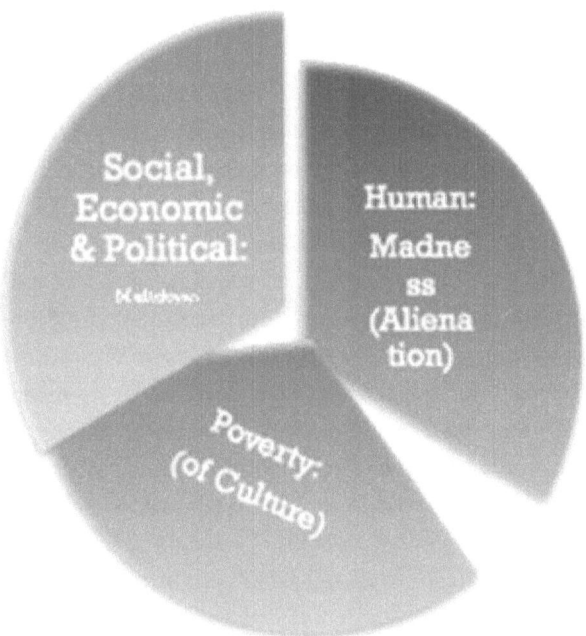

I. Totalization: Banality of 'Oedipalization'

Steven Jobs wrote: "We believe that it's technology married with the humanities that yields us the result that makes our heart sing" (Isaacson, 2011: 527).

In the introduction to <u>Critique of Dialectical Reason</u>[48] Jean Paul Sartre wrote:

---

[48] Published, in the U.S., Published separately as Search for a Method (1968)

"If philosophy is to be simultaneously a totalization of knowledge, a method, a regulative Idea, an offensive weapon, and a community of language, if this "vision of the world" is also an instrument which ferments rotten societies, if this particular conception of a man or of a group of men becomes the culture and sometimes the nature of a whole class-then it is very clear that the periods of philosophical creation are rare...If this movement on the part of the philosophy no longer exists, one of two things is true: either the philosophy is dead or it is going through a "crisis." In the first case there is no question of revising, but of razing a rotten building; in the second case the "philosophical crisis" is the particular expression of a social crisis, and its immobility is conditioned by the contradictions which split society. A so-called "revision," performed by "experts," would be, therefore, only an idealist mystification without real significance. It is the very movement of History, the struggle of men on all planes and on all levels of human activity, which will set free captive thought and permit it to attain its full development (Sartre, 6-8)."[49]

Demythization in the context implies humanization of conscious and unconscious processes which mirror the rise and fall of our cultural, political and religious institutions; totalization represents a mix of objective-subjective, dialectical and analytical reasoning about the duality of existential reality.

A dispassionate discussion on this subject involves a critique of human conditions that 'totalize' psyche. Self, society and state constitute a cultural-structural nexus that incubates human psyche.

---

[49] http://mymill.wordpress.com/2009/09/28/philosophy-as-totalization-of-knowledge/ (April 30, 2012)

Ideological miscegenation—capitalism in China; oligarch in the world's first socialist state, Russia; inequality and racism the US; near anarchic conditions in the world's largest democracy, India etc.—has unleashed bastardized versions of developmental disorders which are unsustainable for any sensible society, let alone an ethical one.

Totalization is not totality. In Sartrean vein, I see totalization as a dialectical process in which praxis tends to totalize human psyche; it's therefore an "overflow" of energy independent of its "envelopment". "Circularity" of this " praxis process " explains the paradoxes that we find puzzling in the ambiguity of twenty-first century (Sartre, 2004; 1968). Sartre, "arguing aprioristically," and losing sight of the individual, contended, "that both individuals and collectives are part of a totalization which produces them and goes beyond them" (Hayman, 1987: 373).

Sartre's obvious 'anti-Oedipus' take on 'totalization' tends to oedipalize power and its mythology.

The cult of war, violence and terror has permeated human society like cancer. A violent society is inherently flawed and deeply implicated in the continued madness that masquerades in different forms. Achieving a society devoid of murder and madness may sound utopian but dystopian positivism has left us without hope[50]. Delusions of guns, god, and greed have dangerously transformed contemporary culture as a totalized reality beyond the power of reason.

Totalization may, contextually, be viewed as a transformative process which seeks dialectical renewal of the human condition. Implicit here is the absurdity of modern existence that thrives on self-destructive neuroses of material outputs devoid of nurturing substance and values. Importantly, it postulates an intuitive, productive and reflective symbiosis between and amongst individuals and society.

---

[50] (See Nietzsche, 1993).

Abstractly, Freud collides with Marx, Marx with Nietzsche, and hope with despair.

In terms of Sartrean ethics, *we are what we make of ourselves.* Our languages, unless they are 'therapeutically' rewritten, are expressions of dominant group values. Nietzsche made it amply clear that 'goodness' did not emanate from altruism. The boundaries that we find between "us" (good; sane; healthy) and "they" (evil; insane; and *the others*) are thus artificial constructs of inane science and troubled humanity.

> "Sartre, Foucault, and Laing have been among the most influential of those who have taught us to distrust the idea of a boundary between sanity and madness and to listen more sympathetically to the "insane" discourse of those who might formerly have been dismissed as incapable of communicating with us." (Hayman, 1987:478).

There is, perhaps, an instinctual element in human creatureliness. Foucault would ask, "How do we ferret out the fascism that is ingrained in our behavior?" (Foucault in Deleuz and Guattari, 1977: xiii). The answer lies in the art of living, Anti-Oedipal quest beyond "neuroticized territorialities" (Seem in Deleuz and Guattari, 1977: xiii; xvii).

Mark Seem comments: "A schizoanalysis schizophenizes in order to break the hold of power and institute research into a new collective subjectivity as a revolutionary healing of mankind. For we are sick, so sick, of our *selves* "(Seem, in Deleuz and Guattari, 1977: xvi). The crux of the problem is best summarized:

> Oedipus is the figurehead of imperialism, "colonization pursued by other means, it is the interior colony, and we shall see that even here at home . . . "This internalization of man by man, this 'oedipalization,' creates a new meaning for suffering, internal suffering,

a new tone of life: the depressive tone . . . ***Depression and Oedipus are agencies of the State, agencies of paranoia, agencies of power, long before delegated to the family. Oedipus is the figure of power as such, just as neurosis is the result of power on individuals. Oedipus is everywhere***"(Seem, in Deleuz and Guattari, 1977: xx; emphasis added)

New Leviathan: Replacing Science, Reason and Humanity

"So, you mock my blindness? Let me tell you this. You [Oedipus] with your precious eyes, you're blind to the corruption of your life . . ." in Oedipus the King, says Tiresias (line, 469)[51].

Discovery of science has indeed transformed the techno-industrial state into an engine of new Fascism, Communism and/or Statist Capitalism. Science will have to be reinvented should we continue to aspire for the goals of the Enlightenment.

Jeff Sharlet in his book, *The Family*, defines *American fundamentalism*, as "a movement that recasts theology in the language of empire" (2008: 3). Religion and politics, in Sharlet's words, "are bound together by the mythologies of America" (2008: 2)[52]. On the other had, the Chongqing model of material success is sadly flawed: "The fall of Bo Xilai signals a change in China's growth-at-any-cost model."(Foroohar, 2012: 22).

---

[51] Sophocles. 1984. Antigone, in *The Three Theban Plays*, trans. Robert Fagles. New York: Penguin.

[52] Lately, Bill Maher, a comedian-intellectual, told one his guests on his HBO show: Half of the Bible is crazy and the other half is wicked (Aril 21, 2012). He added, Whenever a normal person commits an act of horror, religion is always implicated. His guest, a New York Times columnist, hastened to add secular acts of horrors as well.

Human alienation has many faces. Humanity is a dysfunctional joint family. Our interdependence is functionally dysfunctional. We must learn something from bees and primates[53]. The "hive mind," expert on bee behavior says, works like "an exposed brain that hangs quietly from a tree branch" (Zimmer, 2012: 14-15).

> "One of the strengths of honeybees is that they share the same goal: finding a new home. People who come together in a democracy, however, may have competing interests. [Thomas] Seeley advises that people should be made to feel that they are part of the decision-making group, so that their debates don't become about destroying the enemy, but about finding solution for everyone. 'That sense of belonging can be nurtured,' Seeley said. The more we fashion our democracies after honeybees, Seeley argues, the better off we will be." (Zimmer, 2012: 16)

Human society and human nature are not always based on cooperative and collective goals. More often than not, as our history unravels, it's territoriality and conflict that have strengthened the competitive-pugnacious basis of hierarchies and dynasties even within democratic structures. The United States and India are two good examples of *democracies of unfreedom* (Mohan, 1996).

Charles Murray, the controversial author, reexamines "the state of white America' in his new book *Coming Apart* (2012). His thesis is "that the wedge driving America apart isn't its economy but its culture" (Wallace-Wells, 2012: 40). Murray has a point: I argued earlier that poverty is not an economic problem; it's not the culture of poverty, but poverty of culture that breeds despair and inequality

---

[53] "At the end of the day, there is no social interaction of humans that does not bear the imprint of our being a species of animal, or primate, or ape." Robert Sapolsky comments on Games Primates Play (2012)

(Mohan, 2011). I took a global view of the American tragedy. Class still matters; so does our humanity. We are too human to be perfect.

One of the dark ironies of life is that we are becoming lonelier in a wildly interconnected small world[54]. *Facebook* as some experts would have you believe is not "making us lonely" (Marche, 2012: 60-69). The 'epidemic of loneliness' is a product of culture that puts premium on every thing that is non-human. Only two months ago, Time (March 2012: 60-87) offered a stunning analysis of "10 Ideas That Are Changing Your Life"). Eric Klineberg discussed solitary living as "the new norm" (Time, 2012: 60-62).

The dense inter-connectivity of a dangerously networked society is its own nemesis: basic institutions that sustained identity, mutual support, and restorative seclusions—like a weekend picnic, neighborly get together, privacy; "Bowling" (with Robert Putman?)—mark the death of community itself[55]. Is it not a startling fact that young people prefer cohabitation without marriage and the rates of divorce are higher amongst the elderly? When Narcissism becomes expediently profitable, hedonism becomes an expensive luxury with inherent penalties. We are new nomads in a lonely, wild west.

Competition and cooperation have always coexisted with conflicts and compassion. A new reality which is neither functional nor expedient, is rather very self-destructive, selfish and irresponsible. I have always thought of freedom as a call for responsibility. "I am condemned to be free," as Sartre would say. The generation Y is materially wiser; intellectually, selfish and imprudent. Social responsibility became bad words ever since Reagan-Thatcher laid down the foundation of a "market society."

---

[54] 5% U.S. population, according an expert, uses 57% painkillers (Dr Drew on Real Time With Bill Maher, HBO, February 17, 2012.

[55] *See* Robert Putman (2000)

There are tremors in global capitalism. No wonder the "misery index" makes a Darwinian point: "Those at the top of the pecking order have the least stressful and most healthy lives" (The Economist, April 14, 2012: 87). Should this trend continue, it is only going to undergird the foundations of a very divided world. The rise of staggering inequality is not a sustainable index by any standard.

The problem at the top is its unawareness of the forces at the bottom. Chile's "middle class revolt", aftermaths of the Arabian Spring, India's protest against public corruption and self-immolations by Tibetan refugees are strong indicators of the despair people in power seem to ignore. The queen of Syria, ordering perfumes and Harry Potter books while mayhem is rampant outside her palace, reminds us of the fiddling Nero while Rome was on fire. Empires will continue to fall. Temples have seen enough of ruins and destruction and reconstruction.

II. Poverty of Culture: Beyond Terror

New social scientists' diagnosis why civilizations have fallen relate to the "origins of power, prosperity, and poverty" (Acemglu and Robinson, 2012; also, Sachs, 2011). We have known about the origins of inequality since Rousseau both in Marxian and Freudo-Darwinian traditions. There is substantial wisdom in the analyses and analects that we have studied from generations. Still something remains unanswered. My concerns today relate to human appetites that devour our culture of its existential quality.

Modernity greatest myth is that globalization is a product of democratic freedom. I would argue the opposite: Man's madness to conquer the world unleashed the reign of expansionist terror; and, unbridled lust for power and control invented Alexander, Genghis Khan, Napoleon, Hitler, Stalin and Mao Zedong. Ideologies, old and new, are human abstractions of this madness.

The new madness masquerades as a culture war dramatized by perpetual media debates. Corporate trivialization of substance and reality has totalized our subconsciousness to be free form farce and fraudulent information that poisons free discourse. The demise of academic dissent is perhaps the most tragic event of this new century.

About 4012 years ago the seeds of rapacious greed were sowed as a private-public institution[56]. Colonialism was followed by imperialism. The winds of change brought democracy and, of course, globalism. Civilization has taken tremendous strides beyond comprehension.

"Adam Smith denounced the Company as a bloodstained enterprise: 'burdensome', 'useless' and responsible for grotesque massacre in Bengal."[57] If the modern age began with the birth of the East India Company, the trajectory of global capitalism and its consequences depict a new face of "imperialization" and its schizophrenic-devlopmentalism. There are many reasons to be concerned.

In a war game titled 'How the U.S. Lost the Naval War of 2015?', "published recently in *Orbis,* a prestigious journal, Richard Clark says:

> "My greatest fear is that , rather than having a cyber-Pearl Harbor event, we will instead have this death of thousand cuts. When we lose our competitiveness by having all our research and development stolen by the Chinese." (Rosenbaum, 2012: 17)

After 9/11, Clark famously told Americans: "Your government failed you!" He, again, reminds the world of a frightening "weaponsized

---

[56]   *The Economist,* December 17, 2011:109.

[57]   Ibid. 2011:111.

malware"—like *Stuxnet*—which calls for preparations for a new geo-political paradigm (Rosenbaum, 2012: 17)

If there is an iota of possibility in Clark's dystopian fears, Cassandra Syndrome will destroy us before the Chinese attack. The truth is we look for villains to deify our own heroism. Scientific and technological superiority simply galvanize our hubris. It's time that we liberate our psyche from the Chimeras of heroism and serve the people with humility and grace. A culture *Lies* (Coy, Roberts, Einhorn, 2012), hate and terror (Nelson, Leah. 2012[58]) has to be rejected to save us from ourselves.

Modernity and mental illness have one thing in common: A dichotomous banality where the primordial modes of existence coexist with new modes of self-destruction. It's Huxley's Brave New World in which no one wins. Not even the Chinese. Is it not the triumph of Nietzschean *Id*? We may ultimately realize that we are almost nearing a grand collapse[59]."Western nations appear to have fallen out of love with free speech and are criminalizing more and more kinds of speech through the passage of laws banning hate speech, blasphemy and discriminatory language (Turley, 2012)"[60]

---

[58] "A new breed of animal rights activist isn't content with vandalism or arson, but is encouraging deadly acts of terrorism instead" (Nelson, 2012: 22).

[59] A new study from researchers at Jay W. Forrester's institute at MIT says that the world could suffer from "global economic collapse" and "precipitous population decline" if people continue to consume the world's resources at the current pace. In Smithsonian Magazine Australian physicist Graham Turner says "the world is on track for disaster" and that current evidence coincides with a famous, and in some quarters, infamous, academic report from 1972 entitled, "The Limits to Growth."

[60] http://www.latimes.com/news/opinion/commentary/la-oe-turley-criminalizing-speech-20120309,0,3460649.story

Modern existence is a velvety adaptation to reality, which implies masquerades of artificially, sugar-coated as differentially labeled excuses to avoid pain. Again, to quote Jobs, "When you have feelings like sadness or anger about your cancer or your plight, to mask them is to lead an artificial life" (2011: 249). We live in a culture where 'poison' is preferred to 'pain.' It's particularly painful when it melts down motherhood. Judith Warner writes about eloquently:

> *"Manic cookie-baking at midnight. Play dates as complicated as peace summits. Mother-of-the birthday-boy meltdowns. Ambien nights and Ritalin days. No sex. No Nights out. No sleep. Ever..."* (Warner, 2005).

The signs of meltdown are culturally scripted on the canvas of human psyche. In 1917, number of psychiatric disorders included 22 diagnoses; the latest version of DSM now lists 350 (Cloud, 2012: 45). From individual to family to global community, our 'broken windows' seem unsettling from the viewpoint of a social scientist who still believes in humanity's best performances. We live 'agony and ecstasy' muddling through the ambiguities of hope (Mohan, 2012).

The history of human evolution is short and nasty; "95 percent of human history was spent surviving and reproducing—and fighting—in small clans of hunter-gatherers" (Potts and Hayden, 2008: 14). The greatest achievement of this civilization has been the lessons of the Enlightenment. Malcolm Potts and Thomas Hayden are right:

> "Culture evolves more rapidly than biology does, however, which lends hope to the challenge before us: to understand and rein in our Stone Age behaviors." (2012: 15; [61])

---

[61] The rising number and need for sperm banks and donations is a new frontier of man's 'denial of death' (Becker, 1973). A virgin man recently reported having 1000 kids.

How have we come this way? The policies of Rule and Ruin (Kabaservice, 2012) have nearly destroyed the hope for the future. Is it not tragically paradoxical that we shoot each other even in our most guarded and venerated Schools of learning[62]? Our gated communities have become newly segregated living where a colored man dare not walk[63].

Is it not ironic that the rate of suicides is highest amongst the soldiers in US army? Still more worrisome is that there is a staggering disconnect between American pubic and the US military.

What happens if ratio of 1% vs. 99% inequality, like all other commodities of our consumerist culture—are globalized?

Whatever happened to the goals of the Enlightenment, failure of science and reason is a matter of incalculable loss. Academic complacence and arrogance border on a delusional scale if we question the outcomes of the Enlightenment against its avowed mission of totalization of knowledge, truth and reason (Mohan

---

[62]   Campus killings have become so commonplace that many states are legalizing concealed guns in colleges.

[63]   A neighborhood watcher named Zimmerman 'stood his ground' and shot an African American teen-ager because he felt threaten by his presence. While . . . Tryvom, the victim cried for help the aggressor defended 'his right of self-defense' regardless of the obvious implications.

In the labyrinths of this tragedy lies the nexus of gun policies, racism and violence that characterize...A day hardly goes by when insane shootings and random mayhem do not scar the collective face humankind. Our broken school system and fallen family structures have unleashed a perfectly 'incomplete' generation of kids who are lost in the wilderness of their monstrous freedoms. Are they victims of a dysfunctional culture or perpetrators of a new trend in devolutionary cycle? Reports on genocidal barbarity are not too uncommon.

2012). Has our culture become pschopathologically decadent? Or, is it the fatal triumph of the Will to Power?[64]

"Virtue is knowledge, all sins arise from ignorance, and virtuous man is the happy man." This Socratic wisdom has morphed contemporary science and technology into a counterfeit of reason. Can we retransform it? It depends on the direction of a metaphysical hurricane that monstrously hangs over us and we watch its landfall helplessly. There is good news about *Subliminal*: "People informed of the biases and pitfalls of the unconscious brains are better at using their conscious minds." (Modinow, 2012).[65]

The ominous, continued strife against age-old evils remains a madman's Dionysian dream. All we need is 1) historicize; 2) de-idealize; and 3) remember: "To breed an animal with the right to make promises—is not this the paradoxical task that nature has set itself in the case of man? Is it not the real problem regarding man? (Nietzsche, 1967: 57)

The idea of 'ethical society' is an oxymoron; so is the oracle of 'overman.' Hegemonic structures come and go; people remain. Indicators of a global Spring[66] on the world horizon are dim and sparse.

---

[64] As Nietzsche postulated that culture evolved at three levels from Primitive (pure Dionysian) to life-affirming Apolline Dionysian to 'civilized' 'pure' Apollonian. While level one is 'barbarian', the third is a lawfully idealized civilized stage. Contemporary western society, which tends to globalize culture, is pathologically Appolline and decadent (Nietzsche, 1967a).

[65] Cited in *The Economist*, April 28-May 4, 2012: 90.

[66] Yet there are sign of hope: Some 40,000 people converged at a central square in Oslo in the pouring rain to sing the 1970's song "Children of the Rainbow" — a Norwegian version of American folk music singer Pete Seeger's "Rainbow Race." 17Thousands defy Norway mass killer Breivik in song. True, there is one race—human—and its color is rainbow.

In conclusion: We are a psyched up species destined to self-destructive delusions. Aren't we all increasingly leading an "artificial" life? Isn't globalization a poor aping of the decadent culture that thrives on war profiteering, mindless consumption and soul-less exploitation of men, women, children and their *mother* earth? I hope I am wrong (Mohan, 2012).

REFERENCES

Acemglu, Doron and Robinson, James A. 2012. Why Nations Fail: The Origins of Power, Prosperity and Poverty. New York: Random House.

Beech, Hannah. 2012. Murder, Lies, Abuse and Other Crimes of The Chinese Century. Time, May 14: 25-31.

Becker, Ernest. 1973. *Denial of Death*. New York: Free Press.

Cloud, John. 2012. What Counts as Crazy? Time, March 19: 42-45.

Coy, Peter, Roberts, Dexter and Einhorn, Bruce. 2012. The Great Fall of China. Bloomberg Businessweek, May 7-13: 6-8.

Deleuz, G. and Guattari, F. 1977. Anti-Oedipus: Capitalism and Schizophrenia. New York: Penguin,

Deleuz, G and Guattari, F. 1987. A Thousand Plateaus: Capitalism and Schizophrenia. Trans. Brian Massumi. London: University of Minnesota Press.

Farrohar, Rana. 2012. The Party's Over. Time, April 23: 22.

Foucault, M. 1965/1988. Madness and Civilization: A History of Insanity in the Age of Reason. New York: Vintage Books.

Foucault, M. 1977. *Preface* (Deleuze and Guattari, 1977: xi-xiv).

Fromm, Eric. 1982. Postscript, 'Religion and Society'. Funk, R. (1982: 294-295)

Funk, Rainer. 1982. Erich Fromm: The Courage to be Human. New York: Continuum.

Haidt, Jonathan. 2012. The Righteous Mind: Why Good People Are Divided by Politics and Religion. New York: Pantheon Books.

Halleck, Seymour L. 1971. The Politics of Therapy. New York: Science House.

Hayman, Ronalds. 1987. Sartre: A Biography. New York: Simon and Schuster.

Isaacson, Walter. 2011. Steve Jobs. New York: Simon Shuster.

Kebaservice, Geoffrey. 2012. Rule and Ruin: The Downfall of Moderation and the Destruction of the Republican Party, from Eisenhower to the Tea Party. New York: Oxford University Press.

Marche, Stephen. 2012. Is Facebook Making US Lonely? The Atlantic (The Culture Issue). May, 309, 4: 60-69.

Marcuse, Herbert. 1969. An Essay on Liberation. Boston: Beacon Press.

Marcuse, Hebert. 1970. *Five Lectures: Psychoanalysis, Politics, and Utopia.* Trans. J.J. Shapiro and S.M. Weber. Boston: Beacon Press.

Mohan, B. 1992. Global Development: Post-Material Values and Social Praxis. New York: Praeger.

Mohan, B. 1993. Eclipse of Freedom: The world of Oppression. Westport, CT: Praeger.

Mohan, B. 1996. Democracies of Unfreedom: The United States and India. New York: Praeger.

Mohan, B. 1999. Unification of Social Work: Rethinking Social Transformation. New York: Praeger.

Mohan, B. 2005. Reinventing Social Work: The Metaphysics of Social Practice.

Mohan, B. 2007. Fallacies of Development: Crises of Human and Social Development: New Delhi: Atlantic Publications.

Mohan, B. 2011. Development, Poverty of Culture, and Social Policy. New York: Palgrave Macmillan.

Mohan, B. 2012. Agony and Ecstasy: My Omnibus (in press)

Murray, Charles. 2012. Coming Apart: The State of White America, 1960-2010. New York: Crown Forum.

Nelson, Leah. 2012. Negation is Over. *Intelligence Report.* Spring, 145:22-25.

Nietzsche, Friedrich. 1967. (Ed., trans. by Walter Kaufman) The Genealogy of Morals and Ecce Homo. New York: Vintage Books.

Nietzsche, Friedrich. 1967a. (Tr. Walter Kaufmann) Will to Power. New York: Random House.

Nietzsche, Friedrich. 1993. The Birth of Tragedy. (Trans. Shaum Whiteside). London: Penguin Books.

Packard, Vance. 1968. The Sexual Wilderness. New York: David McKay Co.

Potts, Malcolm and Hayden, Thomas.2008. Sex and War: How Biology Explains Warfare and Terrorism and Other Offers a Path to a Safer World. Dallas, TX: Benbella Books.

Putman, Robert D. 2000. Bowling Alone: The Collapse and Revival of American Community. New York: Simon & Schuster.

Rosenbaum, Ron. 2012. Cassandra Syndrome. Smithsonian, April, 12-17.

Sapolsky, Robert. 2012. Games Primates Play. New York: Basic Books.

Sachs, Jeffery D. 2011. The Price of Civilization: Reawakening American Values and Prosperity. New York: Random House.

Sartre, Jean Paul. 2004. Critique of Dialectical Reason Volume I Theory of Practical Ensembles Tr. by Alan Sheridan Smith. New York: Verso.

Sartre, Jean-Paul. 1968. Search for a Method. Translated by Hazel E. Barnes. New York: Vintage Books.

Seem, Mark. 1977. *Introduction,* (Deleuze and Guattari, 1977: xv-xxiv).

Sharlet, Jeff. 2008. The Family: The Secret Fundamentalism at the Heart of American Power. New York: Harper (Perennial).

Szasz, Thomas S. 1970. The Manufacture of Madness. New York: Harper & Row.

Szasz, Thomas S. 1974. The Myth of Mental Illness. New York: Perennial Library.

Wallace-Wells, B. 2012. Return of the radical. Time, April 16: 39-42.

Warner, Judith. 2005. Perfect Madness: Motherhood in the Age of Anxiety. New York: Riverhead (Penguin) Books.

Zimmer, Carl. 2012. Hive Mind. Smithsonian, March, 14-16.

About Co-Editors

 **Sonia Kapur** obtained her Master's and doctorate in sociology from the Jawaharlal Nehru University, India. Her research interests include social stratification, inequality, gender and social development. Dr. Kapur has varied experiences of working in nonprofit sector organizations and on developmental projects across South Asia especially in Afghanistan, Bangladesh, India and Nepal. She is an Assistant Editor of the *Journal of Comparative Social Welfare*, pursuing a second Ph.D. in public policy and teaching courses on gender, policy and politics at the University of Arkansas, Fayetteville, USA

 **Kirpal Singh Soodan,** a professor emeritus at Lucknow University, has extensively published, taught and researched in many a field including aging, social work practice and social research. He is the author, most recently, of *Introduction to Social Work (2008), Social Work Research (2008) and Samajkarya Sidhant aur Abhiyas (2010).* His seminal study, *Aging in India* (Minerva, 1975), is a pioneering work in social gerontology. Dr. Soodan currently lives in Ludhiana, Punjab where has debuted as a novelist, story writer and poet.

 **Usha R. Srivastava** has been on the faculty for more than three decades at Lucknow University (before retiring lately). Having served in many a capacity involving field work supervision and coordination of Post-Graduate Program on Civil Duties and Human Rights, she has lately engaged in an NGO promoting girls' education in rural India. Her teaching and research interests include Social Policy, Women Equality and Empowerment, International Social Development and Social Justice.

In memoriam:

Hilda C.M. Arndt
Rajendra N. Awasthi
Gowind Bhatt
Scott Briar
Eveline M. Burns
Sushil Chandra
Barry M. Daste
Navin C. David
Robert Giles
Russell J. Henderson
Milton Lebowitz
Judith Galbraith Lynam
Prayag D. Mishra
Shital P. Nagendra
Chandi Prasad
Raza
Shushil K. Roberts
Ram Narain Saxena
Sewa Ram Sharma
S.P. Srivastava
Ellison Tyler
Anne & Bernard J. Wiest

&

R. Shree Devi Sharma; Akash, Mayank, and Manisha Sharma; Shushila Devi and Phool Chandra Sharma; Anil Sharma; Nigel Sharma; Nirmala Sharma; Shyam Saran Sharma; Mohan Lal Sharma; Pundit Jwala Prasad Sharma (dada); and Gopi Nagaich

www.ingramcontent.com/pod-product-compliance
Lightning Source LLC
Chambersburg PA
CBHW051441280526
45785CB00003B/1376